MANAGING STRESS

Ursula Markham conducts regular stress management workshops for large organisations and is a practising hypnotherapist dealing with every aspect of stress control in men, women and children.

MANAGING STRESS

THE PRACTICAL GUIDE TO
USING STRESS POSITIVELY

Ursula Markham

ELEMENT BOOKS

First published in 1989 by
Element Books Limited
Longmead, Shaftesbury, Dorset

Phototypeset in 10.5/12pt. Palatino
by Photoprint, Torquay, Devon

Printed and bound in Great Britain by Billings,
Hylton Road, Worcester

Designed by Jenny Liddle

Cover illustration by Peter Till

Cover design by Max Fairbrother

British Cataloguing in Publication Data

Markham, Ursula
Managing stress
1. Managers. Stress
I. Title
658.4'095

ISBN 1–85230–071–X

CONTENTS

To
Philip and David
With all my love

'Farewell the tranquil mind! Farewell content!
. . . That make ambition virtue!'

William Shakespeare (*Othello*)

INTRODUCTION

6.30am: *I must get up early today and go through those notes for this morning's meeting. If only I hadn't been so tired last night I could have done it then. I wish I had been able to sleep better, I'd feel so much more alert.*

8.15am: *I should have left the house twenty minutes ago; the traffic is bound to be heavier now. I must make it on time. I shouldn't have bothered with that tea and toast, it's given me such indigestion.*

9.00am: *Still ten more miles to go. Damn this traffic!*

9.55am: *The board members aren't going to be too happy with these figures. Sales are down; production is down – I just don't seem to be able to motivate the sales team. I wish I didn't feel so shaky, I dare not let them see how nervous I feel.*

12 noon: *Thank goodness that's over – but how dare they go on at me as if it's all my fault! If I had been given more time; a better sales force; a better product . . . How am I supposed to be able to cope with all this?*

1.00pm: *I must get these revised figures sorted out by this afternoon; and I've got a meeting with that idiot Harris at 2.30pm. No time for lunch; I'll just have a bun and a coffee while I work.*

3.00pm: *I've been sitting here listening to him go on and on for twenty minutes now. Not only did he not have the courtesy to be on time but he hasn't even brought all the information with him. This whole meeting is a waste of time. We'll have to set up another one, though I don't know when, my diary is already full.*

4.00pm: *Hello – yes – for heaven's sake, how do I know what time I'll be home? The way things are going I'll be lucky to get away at all! I know we're supposed to go out to dinner with the Martins* *tonight but you'll just have to ring and cancel it, won't you? Good grief, I don't know which day to suggest, I've got more important things on my mind! You just don't seem to realise the way things are round here.*

6.20pm: *Well, that's it. I can't face doing any more now – my head is thumping and the words are dancing around in front of my eyes. I'll just have to take it with me and do it tonight. What I need right now is a drink – I think I'll call in at The Crown before I start for home.*

8.15pm: *I know I'm late – you don't have to go on at me! If the dinner's dried up I'll have a sandwich, I'm not hungry anyway. All I want right now is a large scotch and a bit of peace.*

10.00pm: *I must get down to that paperwork after I've watched the news on television.*

10.30pm: *I'm exhausted. If I have an early night I can get up at six and go through those notes before I leave. I'll just have a quick nightcap.*

2.00am: *I wish I could get some sleep. I'm so tired, but I just keep tossing and turning. I wonder if I handled that meeting well enough today, I hope I didn't make the wrong impression. There's so much to do tomorrow – I don't know how I'll ever catch up.*

6.30am: *I must get up early to go through those notes . . .*

CHAPTER ONE

What is Stress?

Although this chapter is headed 'What is stress?', let us deal first of all with what it is *not*. Stress – today's evil word – is not always the demon king it is made out to be. A certain amount of stress is a necessary, even a beneficial, element in our lives. When the brain registers that a potentially stressful situation exists, we experience a surge of adrenalin, and this in turn can lead to an increase in performance. The caveman was only too pleased to experience this surge of adrenalin when he faced the wild beast, as it gave him the extra strength and speed he needed to make his escape. Today's pedestrian is equally happy to feel that extra charge as he crosses the road and sees a huge heavy goods vehicle bearing rapidly down upon him. After all, that is not the moment to be calm and relaxed. That is the moment to run like hell!

In the same way, that adrenalin surge can give an individual the impetus to be innovative and to think on his feet, or to come up with the best solution to a problem. So it would not be to our advantage to do away with stress and its effects altogether. What we need to do is to nullify the harmful effects of excessive stress on our physical and mental health.

Having demands made upon you – even if they are over and above those you normally have to deal with – does not have to be a source of harmful stress. It can be a challenge to your abilities and, if you are able to rise and meet that challenge, you will actually gain both in skill and self-confidence.

Being anxious about a situation is not the same thing as being stressed. If you are able to recognise that anxiety in yourself, it can serve as an extremely valuable and timely warning that it is time to evaluate a particular situation and decide on an appropriate course of action.

Having a great deal of responsibility placed upon you does not necessarily mean that you will feel the harmful effects of stress. Some people thrive in just such circumstances and produce their best work when they feel completely responsible for the outcome.

In business situations it is often difficult, if not impossible, to reduce the pressure of a high-powered position. Indeed, as the executive moves higher up the ladder, so he becomes more deeply involved in his work and this pressure is likely to increase rather than decrease. The person concerned, however, does not have to suffer any ill-effects, as stress itself causes no harm if kept firmly in its place. What this rising executive, whether male or female, has to do is to make full and beneficial use of his non-working time. Whether he takes up some non-competitive hobby, learns to practise some form of relaxation, takes up exercise, corrects his diet or increases his vitamin intake – any or all of these can help to ensure that he does not suffer any ill-effects.

If you think about it, it is often necessary to pull out the choke in order to start the engine of a car or to give it an extra boost. Damage is only done to that engine if the choke is left out all the time. In the same way, no harm will come to the business executive if he works hard and for quite long hours, provided he counteracts that work by taking regular breaks – whether they be for an hour each day, a day each week, or a holiday every few months. Of course, what he does with that free time is vitally important too.

Everyone reacts to stress in a different way. One man will argue with his wife; another will develop severe backache. One woman will experience pre-menstrual tension; another will start to suffer from migraine. Later in this chapter you will find a list of symptoms caused by excessive stress. Some of them may be what you will expect to find but others may well surprise you. It is very important that you deal with the root cause – the stress itself – rather than just trying to alleviate the symptoms.

In my car there is a little red light which comes on as a warning when something is wrong. It would be somewhat foolish of me to go into a garage and merely ask the man to remove the bulb from that little red light so that it did not come on any more. What I have to do is to have the vehicle checked so that the fault can be discovered and rectified. It would be just as foolish for anyone who can identify with one of the symptoms listed later to resort merely to taking pills and potions to mask that symptom. The only answer is to identify the basic problem – namely the stress in your life – and deal with that.

Sometimes it is necessary for the individual to learn to look at things in a different light. One does not have to become complacent, but there are certain happenings which the individual can do nothing about, yet which we all have to face at some time or another. Everyone is going to experience the shock and grief of a bereavement at some point in his life. There are world events and situations which make us less than happy, but about which we can do nothing. A number of people find that such circumstances add to the amount of stress that they feel and yet, because of our inability to do anything but live with the situation, that stress is often a waste of human energy and potential.

Physical Reactions to Stressful Situations

When the brain informs us that we may have to cope with excessive demands, the following physical changes occur:

- adrenalin starts to flow;
- an increased level of blood sugar is released into the bloodstream;
- there is an increase in the heart/pulse rate and a rise in blood pressure;
- breathing becomes more rapid;
- the muscles tense, preparing the body for action;
- perspiration starts.

To return to our caveman, all these physical effects would give him the extra energy needed to run away from his wild beast. In the case of the pedestrian, he would be more able to dodge the oncoming lorry. But suppose you are in a situation where no physical action is appropriate – what are you going to do with all that excess energy? You cannot run away from your superior, nor can you punch him on the nose (however much you may feel like it!) without the most disastrous effects. If you do not find a method of either harnessing or dispelling this surplus physical energy, you are eventually going to suffer in some way and it will probably cause one of the recognised physical symptoms of stress.

Physical Symptoms of Stress

The following is a list of physical, mental and emotional symptoms which can, of course, have causes other than stress. It is always wise, if you feel that you suffer from any of them, to have a medical check-up. But if, as is often the case, no physical cause for the symptoms can be found, it is likely that stress is to blame.

The list which follows is not intended in any way to frighten the reader, although, if you allow stress to take over your life, you may indeed suffer from one, or probably more than one, of the symptoms. However, it is possible, by using some of the various methods set out in the book, to rid yourself of the problems before they get any worse. Indeed, the very fact that you are reading this book indicates that you are aware of a potentially dangerous situation and are prepared to do something about it.

Breathlessness and/or Palpitations

If you have just run for a couple of miles, you are entitled to feel breathless and there is obviously nothing wrong in this. But if the thought of an important meeting or a disagreement with a colleague is enough to make you short of breath, take heed. And if you lie in bed at night listening to the rapid beating of your heart, and all it seems to do is beat faster and faster as you listen, it is time to do something about it.

Nausea or Vomiting

If either of these symptoms persist you should always seek medical advice. Quite often, however, you will be told that there is nothing physically wrong with you. If this is the case, then you should look at your lifestyle and see whether: 1. you are eating the right sort of foods and 2. allowing yourself enough time to eat and digest your meals. Many businessmen go from one extreme to the other: on one hand you have the company lunch or dinner when more rich food is eaten than necessary; on the other hand there are the days when there is just 'no time to eat' at all. Add to this the tension created by the daily pressure of work, and nausea and vomiting are definitely stress-related.

Dizziness

Does the room seem to spin when you stand up quickly? Do you sometimes feel that you are looking at life through the wrong end of a telescope? Both of these are well-known symptoms of excessive stress.

Asthma

Asthma is *always* emotionally based. As opposed to hay fever – which is a physical allergy – asthma is brought on by feelings of fear, anxiety, emotional upset or tension. Then, of course, the attack seems to take on a life of its own. Because the feeling of being unable to breathe makes this an unpleasant and often frightening complaint, the sufferer is likely to panic and therefore to become even more tense at the first signs of an attack. In this way, the intensity of the attack is increased, as well as the severity and length of time it is likely to continue.

Need (as Opposed to Liking) for Alcohol

There is nothing wrong with the feeling that you would like a drink. But if you get to the stage where you cannot go on without a drink, that is the time to pause and take stock of the situation before the problem grows any bigger. Remember that the definition of an alcoholic is somebody who cannot get through the day without *one drink*.

Excessive Smoking

We all know and understand that smoking is never particularly good for you. It is unpleasant and can be harmful to you and to others around you. Moreover, these days it is becoming more and more anti-social to smoke. However, this section is not intended to preach abstention but to ask you to take a look at your smoking habits. Has the amount of smoking increased drastically lately? Do you smoke because you actually enjoy the taste, or is it because it 'calms your nerves'?

(In fact, of course, it does no such thing. The nicotine actually increases the amount of tension in the body.) Do you find that you tend to 'chain smoke' during important meetings? Is the first reaction to the sound of the telephone ringing to reach for a cigarette? If the answer to any of these questions is in the affirmative, then it is time to ask yourself whether stress plays a greater part in your life than you had realised.

Loss of Appetite

If you find that, even when you think you feel hungry, once you are faced with a meal you have no real desire for it, then stress may well be the cause, particularly if you feel that you cannot eat because your throat feels constricted and swallowing is difficult.

Craving for Food

It might seem strange that both loss of appetite and craving for food can be the results of stress – but it is indeed so. Many children were brought up by well-meaning mothers to look upon food either as a reward for good behaviour or a punishment for bad, so the desire for food is often emotionally based. Looked at in that light, perhaps you will see that it is not so unlikely that the stressed man or woman will seek food as a comfort. The more the tension mounts, the more they will look to food as an escape. Of course, if this craving for food reaches epic proportions, then weight problems may well appear and these will only serve to increase the stress of the sufferer as he will then have something else to worry about.

Insomnia

Here we go back to the analogy of the choke of the car being pulled out. If you have been so stressed during the day that your body has prepared for physical action, only to find that there was after all no outlet for all that energy created within you, then naturally when you try to sleep the excess of adrenalin will still be there. And, of course, the more frustrated you get with the fact that you cannot sleep and the more you try unsuccessfully to go to sleep, the more tense and angry with yourself you will feel, and so the more energy your body will produce.

Nightmares

I mentioned earlier that a certain amount of stress is not harmful provided you know how to 'switch it off'. If you do not find some means of letting go of the stress within you before you go to bed at night, then nightmares or strange dreams will often ensue. Perhaps Scarlett O'Hara in *Gone with the Wind* had the right idea when she used to proclaim, 'I will worry about that tomorrow'. You cannot alter what has already happened and, although planning for the future is both sensible and necessary, once you have made those plans all the worrying in the world is unlikely to improve them.

Constant Tiredness

There is a great difference between the healthy tiredness which one experiences at the end of the day, and that nagging ongoing feeling of exhaustion which never seems to leave you. If you seem to wake tired, even when you know you have slept for many hours; if you feel too mentally exhausted to cope with the tasks you have to face; if you feel yourself to be drained of all energy when you know you have not been over-exerting yourself; then it is more than likely that a build-up of stress is the cause.

Onset of Allergies

The important word here is 'onset'. Many people are born with allergies or develop them as they grow up and these may or may not be stress-induced. But if you suddenly find that you are unable to eat certain foods, tolerate bright lights or touch certain substances, and if your doctor can find no cause for these developments, it is highly likely they are produced by a build-up of stress in your life. As a test, you can try to become aware of whether or not these allergies always seem to get worse when you feel you are under extreme pressure.

Chronic Indigestion

Indigestion, of course, can be a symptom of more serious complaints such as heart trouble, and so it should never be treated lightly. But let us suppose that you have had a check-up and have learned that there is nothing whatsoever wrong with your heart. What is the answer? In very many cases the indigestion is the direct result of stress. When we are dealing with a busy person the problem is often made worse by the fact that he or she feels that there is no time to sit and eat a proper meal, and so either nothing is eaten at all, or a hurried sandwich is gulped down 'on the run' between one stressful situation and another.

Nail-biting

This is perhaps one of the more obvious signs of stress and one which is recognised by almost everyone. Although it may seem relatively trivial, and is certainly not in itself life-threatening, if you bite your nails you should realise that it is an indication of stress and tension within you. Apart from the fact that you probably do not want others to realise how stressed you are – and the bitten nails are a real give-away – it is quite likely that if you are tense enough to bite your nails, there may be other symptoms which you have not considered. Even if this is not the case, it is better to try and deal with the stress before it takes an even greater hold.

Constipation or Diarrhoea

Chronic constipation, chronic diarrhoea and, of course, colitis – which is even more extreme – are all definite symptoms of stress. Naturally we are not talking about the isolated occasion which can happen to anyone, but about the recurring situation which, apart from anything else, will upset the balance of vitamins and minerals within the body and the benefit received from your diet. This in turn can lead to a deterioration in health.

Finger or Foot Tapping

You may think that these two habits are relatively unimportant. Of course you are not going to become seriously ill or die because you are constantly drumming your finger nails on the desk or because you are unable to keep your feet and legs still when you sit in a chair. Yet both of these are significant indications that you are beginning to suffer from stress – and they do tend to irritate other people around you, thereby causing them stress too. Try to observe whether either of these two nervous habits are yours and, if they are, do something about the stress in your life before you suffer from far worse effects.

Headaches/Migraine

Anyone can get the occasional headache but if yours are becoming more and more frequent – and especially if you seem to wake up with a headache – it is time to ask yourself the reason why. Assuming that you have had a check-up (including having had your eyes tested) and no reason for the headaches has been discovered, it is extremely likely that stress is the cause. With regard to migraine, an unhappy and debilitating complaint, there are of course people who are allergic to cheese, wine or chocolate and find that one of these will precipitate a migraine attack. In that case the logical answer is to avoid having cheese, wine or chocolate! In almost all other cases migraine is the direct result of excessive stress and tension and as such can be cured by various techniques including hypnosis and quite often acupuncture – to mention just two. You can also help yourself in the most down-to-earth way: follow the help given in the later chapters of this book, get rid of the tension and you will get rid of the migraine – that is a promise!

Anxiety Attacks

This is one of those complaints more often experienced by women than by men – and do remember that when dealing with business people these days we are talking about women as well as men. The fact that in this book I tend to talk about 'he' or the 'businessman' is not to be taken as an indication that I do not realise how many businesswomen there are – merely that it is uncomfortable to have to write 'he or she' or 'him or her' on every occasion. So, what form do these anxiety attacks take? For some people they are inexplicable surges of panic, accompanied by feelings of breathlessness or racing of the heart. For others they bring feelings of extreme nervous anticipation at the start of the day – nervous anticipation which has no logical explanation. They often go as quickly as they come but nonetheless while they are with you, they are both frightening and unpleasant. They are also a clear indication that you are suffering from stress.

Neck or Backache

One of the first places in the body where extreme tension is felt is in the muscles around the top of the spine and the neck. These muscles are the first to become stiff and painful, and any ache in this area should be taken as a clear warning that you are becoming stressed. Tension in this particular area soon spreads to the jaw, the shoulders, the forehead, the entire spine – and to the temper! A massage may well help to alleviate the symptoms, but unless you do something about the underlying stress, they will soon return.

Ulcers

Often known as 'the businessman's complaint' for obvious reasons. At one time the cause of stomach ulcers was put down to large company lunches or eating the wrong food. Although chronically bad eating habits are obviously unhealthy, the occasional indulgence is unlikely to cause ulcers unless there is an underlying stress problem. All the old treatments of drinking milk and so on will be of no use unless the stress itself is treated, as these are just the same as simply removing the bulb behind that little red light in the car!

Becoming Accident-Prone

Think about this: if you walk along a snowy path treading firmly but without any undue fear or apprehension you are unlikely to fall. The person who is terrified of a fall in the snow tenses every muscle while walking. Because of that tension, the person is far more likely to suffer a fall, and if he does fall, he is far more likely to injure himself than someone who is relaxed and relatively unafraid. In the same way, the individual who is suffering from stress will have tensed all his muscles ready for physical action which does not exist, and because of this unnecessary tension, he is far more likely to have an accident. So, if you have noticed that you are becoming more clumsy, not concentrating as well as you

should, banging into things – and once again, if a medical
check-up has found nothing wrong with you – then stress is
probably the cause.

Eczema or Psoriasis

Both eczema and psoriasis are distressing and extremely uncomfortable complaints. Because they often look unpleasant
they cause embarrassment to the sufferer and in addition he
has to contend with the agonies of constant irritation which
often reach intolerable levels at night. Creams can help to a
certain extent, but they are only masking the symptom
instead of treating the cause. The type of stress-sufferer who
is likely to develop either eczema or psoriasis is the one who
copes so wonderfully well on the surface that nobody would
know he was even feeling tense at all. Many people have
found that when they go into hospital to have the condition
treated it seems to disappear as if by magic. What is
happening, of course, is that the person is being removed
from those things which cause him stress. Because he is out
of reach of day-to-day decisions, he can do nothing about
any situations which may arise – and so the tension eases
and the skin condition disappears.

Addiction to Medication/Drugs

I am not talking here about drugs such as heroin or cocaine,
although addiction to these substances is a real and terrible
form of sickness. What I am referring to is the drugs
prescribed by possibly well-meaning doctors which, after a
short time, actually have no beneficial effect at all but leave
the patient addicted to them. Do you find that you *cannot*
sleep without a pill? Do you need yet others to keep you
going through the day? Are you taking painkillers – whether
prescribed or bought over the counter – for a complaint for
which no physical cause can be found? If you can answer
'yes' to any of these questions, then you are in real danger of
becoming addicted to whatever medication you have been
taking. Now one of the things it is extremely unwise to do in
the case of addiction is to cut out the offending tablets all at

once – the withdrawal symptoms would be too drastic and too distressing. What you should find, however, is that as you deal with the stress you will be able to cut down the tablets little by little until eventually you do not need them at all.

Impotence

This is not unusual for any man on the odd occasion – perhaps when he is extremely tired or when he has had rather too much to drink. If, however, you find that it is happening more and more frequently, then it is quite possible that stress is the cause. It is no coincidence that it is a problem which seems to strike men in middle age. It is not the actual age which is significant but the fact that such men are often finding that they have more responsibility at work, and that the pressures put upon them by their careers cause them to suffer from increased stress.

High Blood Pressure

As I mentioned earlier, when the brain tells the body to prepare for action and all the signs of stress appear, one of these is an increase in blood pressure. When there is no physical outlet for that extra surge in energy the blood pressure remains high. If you repeat this process day after day, and never find time in between to set about deliberately lowering the blood pressure (through something like a relax-ation exercise), it remains high. When I go into companies and conduct Stress Management Workshops for them, I always take with me one of the new electronic units which measure blood pressure and pulse rate. I usually ask for a volunteer or two and take their blood pressure, showing them the figures on the dial. Then I merely take them through a basic relaxation routine such as you will read about in a later chapter and, having done that, I measure their pulse and blood pressure once again. It is *always* markedly lower. In this way I am able to prove to those who attend the workshops that it is possible to learn quite simple techniques which will help them to overcome the effects of stress. In just the same way, if high blood pressure is a condition from which you suffer, you can learn to lower it at will and thereby to prevent it causing you real and permanent harm.

Anger/Violence

Very few people will admit to being in any way violent. Extreme stress, however, can lead to such a build-up of anger that for some, violence is almost the only release. Because such people understandably suffer the most dreadful feelings of guilt after the event, the stress from which they already suffered can increase a hundredfold. But, violence apart, it is not at all unusual for a stress sufferer to begin to have extreme outbursts of anger despite the fact that previously his temper might have been neither better nor worse than that of anyone else. This is particularly true in the case of someone who feels that, because of his position, he is not able to express his feelings or release his frustrations at work for fear of incurring the wrath of his superiors. It is a good thing for the individual to find a way of releasing all that pent-up energy – but he would be far better to work it off by digging the garden, running a couple of miles or concentrating on a relaxation exercise, than by allowing himself to become angry with those around him, possibly causing irreparable harm to his relationships with others.

Phobias

Some people develop phobias from a very early age and, although these are totally curable by hypnosis, and sometimes by other methods, this is not what I am referring to here. Those who suffer from stress will sometimes find that they 'suddenly' develop phobias about things which have never caused them any particular problem in the past. To discover suddenly that you have a phobia about flying, for instance, is not unknown in the case of someone who is suffering from a great deal of tension. Often it is not flying itself which causes the irrational fear, but the subconscious knowledge that a great deal is expected of you when you arrive at your destination and that you will be under even more pressure than before. I knew one Department Manager who suddenly found that he had a phobia about dogs when he had never had one before. In fact, he had even had his own dog as a child. Eventually it was discovered that the barking of dogs was linked in his subconscious mind with the harsh temper of his immediate superior. As he did not dare to show his real feelings at work, his mind had found another outlet for his anxiety and had transferred those fears, first of all to the sound of barking, and later even to the presence of a dog. The mind can play all sorts of tricks on us and this is why it is so important to release stress before it can do you any real harm. If you do already suffer from a stress-induced phobia, however, there is no need to despair, as this too can be successfully dealt with and eradicated.

Strokes

How many times have you heard of a business executive who has worked his way up the corporate ladder only to find that when he is nearing the top rung, he suffers a massive stroke. He is then unable either to continue with his work, or even enjoy the fruits of his earlier labours. Indeed, if you look at the charts at the end of this chapter, you will see that the instance of such happenings is higher among Company Directors than for any other profession. This is not intended as a 'doom and gloom' prediction: it does not *have* to happen. It is only recently that strokes have been definitely linked to stress of one sort or another, and so it is only comparatively recently that anyone has even considered taking preventive action. As you have been forewarned of this possible danger, you still have time to learn to control that stress before it controls you.

Heart Disease

You have been reading a somewhat gloomy list of the problems which could arise if you allow stress to be your master. These problems, either singly or in combination, could well lead to a heart attack if not checked. Indeed, well-known cardiologists have come up with a list of personality traits which would indicate that a particular individual is predisposed to heart disease. Look at this list and see how many of the items apply to you. Do you:

- Set yourself impossible deadlines?

- Take on several jobs at one time?

- Walk and talk very quickly?

- Find that you have eaten your meal more quickly than your companions?

- Have a burning sense of ambition?

- Find that you are unable to sit still and that you fidget a great deal?

If you can answer 'yes' to most of these questions then it is time to take yourself in hand. By changing your pattern of life it is possible to reduce the likelihood of coronary disease with all its distressing effects.

Cancer

It is now widely accepted in medical circles that, in the majority of cancer cases, stress is a contributory factor. Of course there are people who have smoked sixty cigarettes a day for years (although perhaps it was stress which made them smoke so much in the first place), just as there are others who have worked with highly abrasive substances over long periods of time, and so when such people develop cancer, perhaps it is more easy to understand. In very many cases, however, the cancer arises because the individual has been totally unable to cope with stress and tension in his life. He may well have coped wonderfully on the surface, while all the time, the damage was being done underneath. If we go back about two years in the life of any new cancer sufferer (assuming that he does not belong to one of the earlier groups I mentioned) and we look at what has been happening to him, we will usually find that there has been some major cause of stress. Sometimes it will have been an unexpected divorce, sometimes a bereavement; perhaps the loss of a large contract or even the threat of redundancy. This does *not* mean that anyone who suffers from one or more of the above problems will necessarily develop cancer. It just means that there are certain people, particularly those who have a tendency to suffer from stress under normal circumstances, for whom one or more of these events will prove to be the last straw. It is possible these days to cure some cases of cancer by a combination of diet, therapy and visualisation – but it is far better to prevent it occurring in the first place. No one is going to go through life without, at some point, suffering the loss of a loved one. Sadly, many people are going to experience the trauma of a divorce or some other personal emotional tragedy. However, provided the individual has learned how to release stress before it does him any harm, then the effects of these and other problems can be overcome without doing him any lasting damage.

Causes of Stress

In the previous section we looked at the symptoms of stress in the hope that you would be able to recognise them in yourself before they could cause you any real and permanent harm. Now let us examine what causes these symptoms in the first place. In other words, what is it that makes us stressed? If we can identify the probable causes of stress we are far more likely to be able to take preventive action before the problem escalates out of all proportion.

More stress is actually caused by anticipation than by the events themselves. Fear of being late and missing an important appointment; fear of not making a sale; fear of being thought of as a failure. Often the event itself never happens and all is well – but the internal damage has already been done. If you are someone who lives in permanent fear of what *might* go wrong, you could be doing yourself very real harm – and all for nothing. Instead of being anxious about possibly missing an important meeting, try to ensure that you leave with plenty of time to spare. If something happens which is totally beyond your control – a delayed flight, or the break-down of a car, for example – then all the worrying in the world is not going to change it. All you can do is deal with each situation which arises in as calm and logical a way as you can.

Anger, frustration or unhappiness over the past can also be a major cause of stress – and yet what a useless one! It may be that you had an unhappy and an underprivileged upbringing; perhaps your parents or a former spouse never really cared for you; or possibly you did something earlier in your life which now you deeply regret. The only time that looking back on such episodes in your past is valuable is if it makes you a little wiser or more understanding in the present and in the future. You cannot change what has gone before, and yet you would be amazed at the number of people who destroy a major part of their adult life by continually dwelling on what happened years earlier. So accept the past for what it was. It is even possible that people and events which caused you to be unhappy in the past have been responsible for making you the person you are today. Perhaps you would not have achieved all that you have, had it not been for them. Unkindness in earlier life often leads to increased tolerance in the former sufferer. Deprivation can lead to a higher appreciation of what one actually achieves for oneself. So acknowledge your earlier life, and then keep it firmly where it belongs – in the past.

Many people are caused very real stress by the daily intrusion of excessive noise, heat or crowds. To others this does not appear to be a problem at all. If you do feel that these things create tension and irritability within you, you must try and do something about it before the problem gets out of control. In an ideal world you would be able to escape from such situations, but we all know that this is just not possible. You must realise, however, that the stress caused by noise and so on is more than doubled when you allow your own anger and frustration to grow. It is far better to acknowledge that you do not really like the situation, and then to make the best of it until you can find some peace again. In addition, by following some of the techniques set out later in the book, you will be able to 'switch off', to become unaware of the noise or of the hordes of people around you, and thus to calm your shattered nerves.

Travel, particularly driving, is another cause of stress. You have to deal with the time it now takes to get from A to B (particularly in city centres), the frustration of traffic jams, motorway repairs and one-way systems – and of course all the other idiots on the road! If you live or work in one of the major cities, however, you will know in advance that your journey will be slow and laborious, so you might just as well accept it and allow plenty of time. Why not make use of that time spent behind the wheel of your car? You could listen to music, plan your next holiday, or you could even do a couple of breathing exercises when you stop at the next red traffic light! When another car suddenly changes lane right in front of you or pulls out from the kerb without signalling properly, what beneficial effect to *anyone* is achieved by sounding your horn, shouting out of the window or even silently letting your temper (and your blood pressure) rise? It is not going to hurt the offending driver; he has already made his move, whether deliberately or accidentally. It is not going to change the situation which now exists. It is certainly not going to help you to drive better or to reach the end of your journey in a calm and reasonable state of mind. So, not only are you likely to do yourself actual damage because of the stress you have caused, you are far less likely to make rational and profitable decisions when you arrive at your destination.

Allowing problems in your personal relationships to overlap into your business life (or vice versa) can be another major cause of stress. The man or woman does not exist who, however happy within a relationship, is not going to have a disagreement with his partner. The business does not exist which is not going to go through a bad patch from time to time. It is quite possible to cope with either of these situations if they are kept firmly in their proper places. But when a couple have a disagreement over the breakfast table and one partner leaves for work inwardly fuming, you can be sure that he or she is not going to be able to put their best effort into the day ahead. If the businessman has had a trying time at work and does not leave his frustrations behind him at the office, he is unlikely to spend a happy and loving evening with his wife when he reaches home. It is vitally important to learn to switch off these feelings of anger or tension when changing from one situation to another or you can end up with two unhappy environments instead of one!

Women in business suffer from a particular form of stress. In many cases not only do they have to work even harder than men to achieve any sort of status within a company but, having got there, they have to deal with the problem of some (though by no means all) of their superiors who still maintain the old prejudices about businesswomen. In addition to this they often have to contend with their own guilt in relation to the blending of business and family life. If a woman has chosen to pursue a career rather than to have children, the media will ensure that she is made to feel guilty and unnatural. Even if she knows in her heart that this is not true, it can still be a major cause of stress. So can the mental juggling she will have to do to make life run smoothly if she has chosen to have a family and a career at the same time.

Some business situations are potentially stressful and whether they affect you or not depends, first of all, upon your personality and, secondly, on whether or not you *allow* them to dominate your thinking. Such things as:

- a heavy workload or a desk full of papers – you can only take care of one thing at a time and, should you allow tension to build up, you will actually deal with each job far less efficiently;

- lack of support from superiors;

- demands put upon you by different people which seem to conflict so that there is no way of pleasing everyone;

- uncomfortable surroundings – perhaps the lighting is poor or the conditions cramped;

- coping with new technology – and there seems to be a constant influx of new equipment and, no sooner have you learned to master one machine, than another one appears on the scene;

- making presentations or attending meetings – will you say the right thing, will you achieve what you set out to do?

- managing or supervising others; having to reprimand when necessary; motivating others to achieve greater success;

- a working relationship with colleagues which is less than satisfactory.

Some people will find the above situations a challenge – which is a positive way of approaching them. Others will consider them threatening – which, of course, is negative. If you are in the position to change any of the circumstances which cause you stress, then it will be in your interest to try to do so. When there is nothing to be done you have two choices: you can change where you are working or you can change the way in which you allow it to affect you. The important word is 'allow'. Even situations we do not like can be tolerated with a certain degree of serenity if we will only make the effort.

Remember too that stress is cumulative. No one isolated situation is going to turn you into someone suffering from the effects of stress. Nor is one temporary setback going to cause you any real harm. It is only when you allow one problem to build up on another without doing anything to counteract it until you have a whole mountain of them, that you are likely to suffer.

The charts which follow are compiled from recent figures taken from the Registrar General's Occupational Mortality Tables and will show you very clearly which occupations are most at risk. They are not meant to frighten you or to indicate the inevitable. All this can be changed. If you will learn, and practise, some of the exercises in this book and make some of the necessary changes in your life and your attitudes, you can make sure that it never happens to you. You try to prevent dental decay by cleaning your teeth; you hope to avoid problems with your car by having it serviced regularly; just look upon this book as another method of prevention – and one which can save your life.

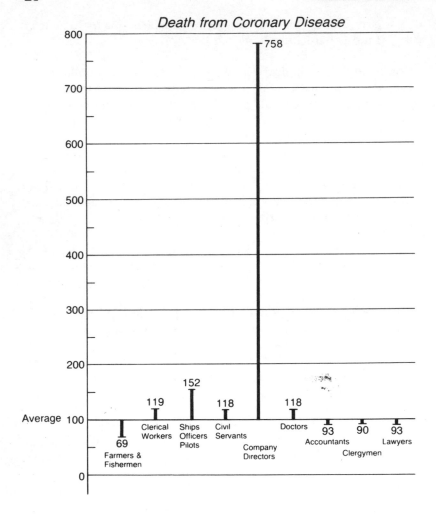

Death from Coronary Disease

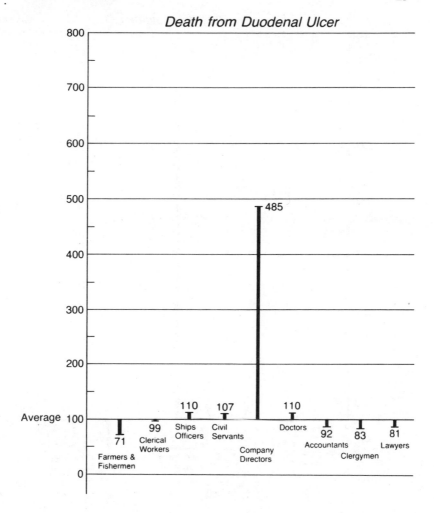

Death from Duodenal Ulcer

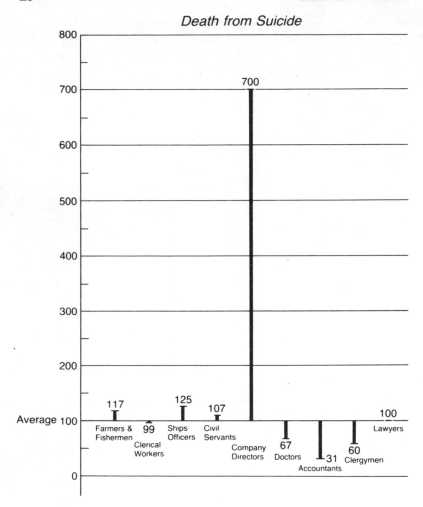

Death from Suicide

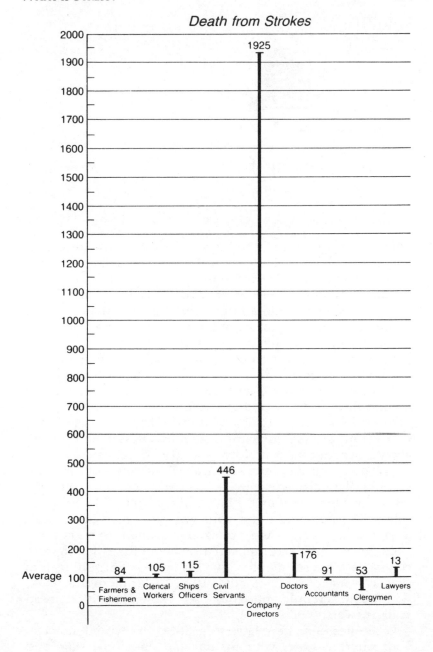

Death from Strokes

CHAPTER TWO

Know Yourself

There is no point at all in trying to deal with your stress until you know precisely how stressed you are at the moment. When I conduct my workshops, it is not at all unusual for people to insist that they are not particularly stressed – it is just that they have had a little more difficulty than usual in getting to sleep lately or have found that they are becoming more irritable with the family! It is only when these same people are made to sit down and weigh up their present condition that they begin to realise how much effect stress is having on their lives – and thereby on the lives of those around them at home and at work.

The questionnaires which follow will enable you to judge how greatly stress is affecting you at the present time. Think about each question in turn and try to be as honest as possible in your answers – after all, if you are not then you will only be harming yourself. You will see that after each question there are four columns. Place your ticks today in column 1. Column 2 is for your answers about one month after starting your own stress management programme. Column 3 should be completed after about three months and column 4 after six months. If you have been putting into practice some of the methods outlined later on in this book, you should certainly notice quite a considerable difference in your answers.

Each questionnaire relates to a different area in your life: your physical state, your mental and emotional state and your stress factor in relation to your work.

Study the questions and place a tick in the relevant column if the answer is 'yes': not if the symptom only occurs occasionally, but if you find that it often arises or – and this is even more significant – if it has recently been more in evidence than ever.

Think hard before answering. If you are at all unsure about the situation regarding yourself and your susceptibility to stress then try to observe yourself in a detached way over the next week or two. Above all be honest with yourself. It is the easiest thing in the world to fool ourselves when we really want to. If, when you come to the end, you find that you have more than three ticks in any questionnaire, then be assured that it is time to do something about it.

1. Assessing your Physical Stress-Factor

	TODAY 1	AFTER ONE MONTH 2	AFTER THREE MONTHS 3	AFTER SIX MONTHS 4
Do you get frequent headaches?				
Do you suffer from tension in your back and neck muscles?				
Do you get pains in your chest?				
Do you suffer from pains in your arms and legs?				
Do your eyes feel tired?				

	TODAY 1	AFTER ONE MONTH 2	AFTER THREE MONTHS 3	AFTER SIX MONTHS 4
Are your eyes often sore and bloodshot?				
Do you have difficulty in getting to sleep?				
Do you wake during the night?				
Do you suffer from disquieting dreams or nightmares?				
Do you have difficulty waking in the morning?				
Do you still feel tired when you wake?				
Do you suffer from impotence?				
Do you suffer from PMT?				
Do you have problems with sexual intercourse?				
Do you suffer from constipation?				

	TODAY 1	AFTER ONE MONTH 2	AFTER THREE MONTHS 3	AFTER SIX MONTHS 4
Do you suffer from diarrhoea?				
Are either of the above more obvious just before an important event?				
Have you lost your appetite?				
Do you have an excessive craving for food?				
Do you have an excessive craving for sweet foods?				
Do you suffer from indigestion?				
Do you *need* a daily drink?				
Has your smoking increased?				
Do you have difficulty in breathing deeply?				
Do you get tired for no obvious reason?				

	TODAY 1	AFTER ONE MONTH 2	AFTER THREE MONTHS 3	AFTER SIX MONTHS 4
Do you sweat excessively?				
Do you find it difficult to sit still?				
Do you have many nervous habits (drumming fingers etc.)?				
Have you been losing your temper more often recently?				
Do little things irritate you?				
Do you bite your nails?				
Do you have dizzy spells?				
Do you feel the desire to cry?				
Do you often suffer from feelings of nausea?				
Do you have sensations of inexplicable panic?				

	TODAY 1	AFTER ONE MONTH 2	AFTER THREE MONTHS 3	AFTER SIX MONTHS 4
Do you have high blood pressure?				
Does your heart seem to race?				
Does your heart seem to miss a beat?				

2. Assessing your Mental/Emotional Stress Factor

	TODAY 1	AFTER ONE MONTH 2	AFTER THREE MONTHS 3	AFTER SIX MONTHS 4
Has your memory grown worse?				
Do you have difficulty concentrating for any length of time?				
Do you dislike yourself?				
Are you apathetic towards life?				

	TODAY 1	AFTER ONE MONTH 2	AFTER THREE MONTHS 3	AFTER SIX MONTHS 4
Is it difficult to generate enthusiasm?				
Are you shy and awkward with others?				
Do you find it impossible to relax?				
Have you lost your sense of humour?				
Are you often anxious?				
Do you have illogical fears?				
Do you find it difficult to display emotion?				
Is it hard for you to show physical affection?				
Do you find it difficult to tell another person how you feel?				
Do you often feel unable to cope?				

	TODAY 1	AFTER ONE MONTH 2	AFTER THREE MONTHS 3	AFTER SIX MONTHS 4
Are you often restless?				
Do you fear the future?				
Are you frightened of being ill?				
Are you afraid of dying?				
Are you upset by ill health in others?				
Do you have a low opinion of yourself?				
Do you feel guilty about the past?				
Do you consider yourself a failure?				
Do you find it hard to make decisions?				
Do you suffer from suppressed anger?				
Do you feel you have been let down by others?				

	TODAY 1	AFTER ONE MONTH 2	AFTER THREE MONTHS 3	AFTER SIX MONTHS 4
Are you misunderstood?				
Do you feel that others dislike or ridicule you?				
Are you generally anxious?				
Do you move on to something new before completing the old task?				
Do you lack confidence?				
Are you nervous with strangers?				
Do you like to do several things at once?				
Do people expect more of you than it is possible to give?				
Are you often the scapegoat for others?				
Do you feel oppressed in enclosed spaces?				
Do you feel anxious in open spaces?				

3. Personality Assessment

(taken from the work of Sharpe and Harper)

First of all, please read through the following list and tick the questions to which you can honestly answer 'yes'.

1. I find it difficult to say 'no' to any kind of demand on me.

2. I get restless if I am not involved in several different activities.

3. I would describe myself as a dedicated type of person.

4. 'A place for everything and everything in its place' is my motto.

5. Disagreements with people really upset me a lot.

6. I like to make a thoroughly good job of all that I do.

7. I get bored very easily.

8. I like to see things through whatever the obstacles.

9. I believe you can only get ahead by taking risks.

10. I find it very hard to take or give criticism.

11. My personal standards are high and demanding.

12. I go for long periods thinking only of one ambition.

13. I think everyone is given just one real chance somewhere in life.

14. I dislike having my daily routine interrupted.

15. I have great difficulty in leaving situations when I have had enough.

16. Months can often go by before I realise I have not seen my friends.

17. I usually put myself second in family matters.

18. I believe it is essential to speculate in order to accumulate.

19. Imperfections of any sort upset me considerably.

20. Work is its own reward.

21. I am impulsive in my relationships.

22. I would rather have one too many appointments in my diary than one too few.

23. I find it difficult to express my needs to others.

24. I am often preoccupied when those close to me are having fun.

25. My motto is, 'Faint heart never won fair lady'.

26. The people I work with know that when I say a thing I mean it.

27. I have very little or no privacy in my life.

28. I dislike having loose ends at work or at home.

29. Sex plays a very secondary part in my life.

30. I become very agitated if people fail to carry out simple instructions.

31. I always seem to lose arguments.

32. I often have difficulty finishing off what I have started.

33. I think the best part of an affair is the thrill of the chase.

34. Being bound up in the day's events often spoils sex for me.

35. I find it difficult to introduce myself and make relationships.

36. I sometimes wonder if I have missed out on relationships by working so hard on my career.

37. I do not find it easy to express my emotions.

38. I tend to worry just as much whether the problem is a large one or a small one.

39. As soon as I have reached one career goal, I set up a higher one.

40. I have sometimes spoiled relationships by having too much going on at once.

How to Score

Type 1 Score one point if you have answered 'yes' to the following questions: 1, 5, 10, 15, 17, 23, 27, 31, 35, 37.

Total: _____ points

Type 2 Score one point if you have answered 'yes' to the following questions: 4, 6, 11, 14, 19, 24, 28, 30, 34, 38.

Total: _____ points

Type 3 Score one point if you have answered 'yes' to the following questions: 3, 8, 12, 16, 20, 22, 26, 29, 36, 39.

Total: _____ points

Type 4 Score one point if you have answered 'yes' to the following questions: 2, 7, 9, 13, 18, 21, 25, 32, 33, 40.

Total: _____ points

You now have four totals – one for each 'type' described below.

A score of 5 or more in any one section would indicate that you fit into the personality type for which that score was obtained.

A score of 8, 9 or 10 in any one section would indicate that you may now or in the future experience some of the stresses listed below for that type.

High scores in more than one section would indicate a high risk of stress responses.

Psychologists have determined that there are four types of individual who are more vulnerable than most to stress at work. These are:

Type 1: Unassertive

These people, who find it difficult to say 'no', can easily slip into situations where they are stressed by demands made on them by those tasks which they have too readily agreed to undertake. They may be made anxious, exhausted or even phobic by this high level of demand made upon them. As they are reluctant to voice their resentment, they may also fall victim to depression and inner conflict. They can sometimes suffer from boredom, having entered jobs which they know will not really provide a challenge or a stimulus. Such people are likely to be over-sensitive and lacking in confidence, and are frequently unable to carry a task through to completion unless pushed.

Type 2: Obsessional

These are people who can cope happily and efficiently with demanding jobs, providing all the tasks involved are predict-able and stable. Such people tend to be particularly fond of all the little traditions, details and rituals of the job. They are often extremely conscientious, competent and hard-working. Should there be a sudden change in the job, however (even a change for the better, such as promotion) or should the work load increase beyond a certain level, not only may they become even less flexible than they were previously, but they may well also develop various typical stress-related physical illnesses.

Type 3: Stimulus-Seeker

These people are the complete opposite of those described as 'Obsessional'. They seem to feel secure only when things around them are changing. Pathologically stimulus-seeking, they will go from one potentially demanding and exciting occupation to another – often involving themselves in either physical or financial risk. Alternatively they may try to re-organise an otherwise conventional job so that it involves cutting corners, taking chances and winning temporary triumphs. Such individuals are in great danger of becoming addicted to stress-induced adrenalin and noradrenalin. This addiction is as real as one involving any other habit-forming external substance. Stimulus-seekers may also get them-selves into situations from which they find it impossible to escape. They are more likely to become heavy smokers and alcohol drinkers or to suffer from symptoms of mental or physical illness.

Type 4: Ambitious

People who are compulsively busy, aggressive and impatient are likely to encounter a number of work-related stresses, most of which they will in fact have initiated themselves. These may be reflected in a wide range of minor illnesses from which they tend to suffer such as migraine, skin complaints and ulcers. Most significantly, however, they are also particularly prone to high blood pressure and heart disease. The frequency and severity of this stress response and the widespread incidence of this type of behaviour – particularly among senior managerial and supervisory executives – has invited a great deal of attention recently.

Types A and B

Two cardiologists, Dr Meyer Friedman and Dr Ray Rosenman, while conducting their researches into the effects of stress upon the heart, divided people into Type A and Type B. Type A are three times more likely to have a stroke or a heart attack than those in the Type B category, even if they are doing the same sort of work and living in similar conditions. Study the lists below and see whether you are a Type A or a Type B. You should not worry if a few of the characteristics of Type A apply to you, but if you can identify with more than half of them, you would do well to try to change some of your responses to those of a Type B individual. This is not impossible and it is never too late to start – particularly if by doing so you can avoid the more serious effects of the stress-induced illnesses.

Type A	Type B
Very competitive.	Not competitive at work or at play.
Strong, forceful personality.	Has an easy-going manner.
Does everything quickly.	Goes about things slowly and methodically.
Strives for promotion at work or for social advancement.	Is fairly content with present position at work and socially.
Wants public recognition for his efforts.	Has no desire for public recognition.
Is easily angered by people and events.	Slow to be aroused to anger.
Feels restless when forced to be inactive.	Enjoys periods of idleness.
Speaks quickly.	Speaks slowly.
Thrives on doing several things at the same time.	Is more content when doing things one at a time.
Walks, moves and eats quickly.	Is unhurried in walking, moving and eating.
Feels impatience at any delay.	Patient and not upset by delay.
Extremely conscious of time – revels in having to meet deadlines.	Not time conscious – ignores deadlines.
Always arrives on time.	Is often late.

Type A	*Type B*
Has taut facial muscles and clenches fists often.	Has relaxed facial muscles and does not clench fists.

Now that you have had a chance to look at the various lists and questionnaires, you will have more insight into yourself and your susceptibility to stress. The next stage is to set about doing something to improve the situation.

Finding Solutions

Set yourself realistic goals. There is no way that a harassed, over-worked executive is going to become an easy-going 'laid-back' type overnight – if ever. You are looking for improvements, not miracles. Any improvement which is to be long-lasting and worthwhile must be achieved gradually. The habits of a lifetime are not going to be set aside in an instant, but there is no reason why you cannot start *now*.

Let us begin by considering the work situation in general. Look at the list which follows and then decide which of the situations described there you find most stressful. Number them all in order of importance.

Being over-loaded with work.
Working to deadlines.
Travelling: to, from and in the course of work.
Having to take work home.
Managing or supervising others.
Difficulties with superiors/other board members/partners.
Lack of communication at work.
Inability to delegate.
Difficulty in disciplining others.
Attending meetings.
Administration and paperwork.
Office politics.
Effects of work on home and family life.

Although you may not be able to eradicate some of the problems mentioned above, it should certainly be possible to ease the situation in regard to each and every one of them. In the case of those where you have comparatively little control over the situation, it is certainly possible to learn to control how much stress that situation causes *you*.

Treat the whole matter as you would do for any business problem which might arise. First of all you have to identify the nature of the problem; this you have already done by checking the list of stressful situations. Now you must decide on a possible solution (or several possibilities if they exist). For example, if your number one problem is the stress caused to you by travelling, perhaps it would be worth your while starting work a little earlier or finishing a little later, thereby avoiding the traffic jams as much as possible. If you find that attending meetings is your greatest cause of stress, even if you cannot avoid these altogether, you can ensure that you are well prepared, are there early and that you practise some of the techniques you will read about further on in the book.

Next you must make a commitment about when you are going to start doing something about the problem. It will not just go away and, if it is already causing you stress, you may be sure that the stress will increase rather than decrease. So start *now*!

As in business, if you want to achieve anything at all you have to identify your goals and how you are going to attain them. Many people find it helpful to create goal-setting cards. Before you say, 'Oh no – not more pieces of paper for me to deal with', get your priorities right. If you do not deal with this particular piece of paper, you may well find that the day will come when stress has created such problems for you, that you are not able to deal with any pieces of paper at all.

So, now that you have decided that you are worth helping, why not make some of these cards for yourself. Ordinary 6" × 4" cards are quite suitable for this.

Problem
Possible solutions: 1.   2.   3.
When (your commitment):
Result:

Create a card like that for the problem you chose as number one on your list. Work on your possible solutions and note the result. Take your time and make it a habit; let it become part of your nature and then you will know that the results achieved will be permanent. Then continue on to problem number two.

As you gradually acquire a pile of cards showing your success in different areas, you will have the satisfaction of knowing that each time you manage to eradicate a potentially stressful situation you are taking another step towards improving the quality – and possibly also the length – of your life.

CHAPTER THREE

Changing Your Lifestyle

'Nonsense,' you may say, having noted the title of this chapter, 'there is nothing I can do to change my lifestyle'. Nevertheless, understandable as this reaction may be, this statement is not true for you any more than it is for anyone else. You *can* change the pattern of your life in many small but significant ways. It just takes a little thought on your part. Naturally I can quite understand that you may not be able to make dramatic changes in your job itself, but you would be surprised at how often it is possible to make minor changes, and thereby save yourself a great deal of unnecessary stress. Also, as this book progresses you will see that it is certainly possible to make very real changes in the *effect* that your work has on you.

Let us begin by considering your working life and seeing what can be done to ease the situation there. The following are some of the greatest causes of stress at work, and some of the possible solutions.

Delegating

We would all like to think that we are indispensable and so our first reaction on being asked whether or not we could delegate some of the tasks we normally handle ourselves, is one of shock and horror to think that anyone else could possibly do things as well as we do. It is very satisfying to think that the business would go into a state of collapse if we are not there to play our part – but this is very rarely true. After all, if you were to become ill (whether because of stress or for any other reason) the world would continue to revolve as would the wheels of business. Even if you were to die, it is unlikely that the business would collapse and fail completely.

Ask yourself whether there are not some tasks you could delegate to others. If your immediate reaction is to answer 'no', ask yourself what would happen if you were incapacitated in some way – how would the business survive? Many people jealously guard the tasks which are theirs, often with disastrous results in the face of an emergency. If it is your own business and you are unable to work for a period of time, do you really want to think that all your efforts will have been in vain and that, by the time you recover, there will be no business for you to run? Of course you don't. However, the time to consider how best to ensure this is not when you are lying in some hospital bed – but *now*. What are you going to do to ensure that, even if your business did not greatly expand in your absence, it would continue to tick over quite nicely.

Suppose the business is not your own but that you are a senior executive in a company. Do you really think that if you were compelled to have a considerable period of time away from work because of illness or accident, the corporate world would come to an end and no one else would be able to do your job? If so, it must be an interesting fantasy world in which you live. The reality of the situation, of course, is that there is always someone else to do every job, whatever it may be. If you find this concept disturbing or distressing, perhaps there is even more reason to take care of your health by refusing to allow stress to affect you. That way you will always be there to do your job, and do not have to fear that it will be taken over by someone else.

So, now that we have decided that other people are capable of doing at least some of the minor tasks you normally do for yourself – and now that we know that you wish to preserve your health and well-being by avoiding stress – it is time for you to sit down and work out which tasks may satisfactorily be delegated to others. This may initially take up more of your time rather than less, especially as you may have to explain particular methods and tasks to those who know little or nothing about them (could this be because you have never allowed them to know?). The time saved by you, however, will in the long run be considerable. That time can then be used either to shorten your working day, or to give you the opportunity to cope more efficiently and more speedily with those tasks which only you are in a position to deal with. Whichever is the case, you will certainly find that you are under less pressure.

Your first step, therefore, is to make a list of any tasks you feel that it is possible to delegate and then of the person you think will be most likely to undertake any or all of those tasks efficiently. There is no point in trying to relieve pressure by allocating a job to someone you do not trust to carry it out as you would like. Far from saving yourself stress, you would be creating a great deal more by worrying about the outcome, and you would perhaps put yourself under even more pressure by feeling that you have to check on everything that person has done.

Travel

No one can deny that travel can be an extremely stressful business, and it is becoming more so with the increase in the amount of traffic on the roads. Yet, even in this area of your life, you may find that you are able to make some significant changes.

How do you travel to work each morning? Perhaps you take your car. The first thing to consider is whether or not it is essential that you have your car at work every day. For some people there is no alternative. If you know that you have to make several journeys by car during the day or if you live in an area where public transport is unreliable, then it may be that you cannot avoid having to drive to work. Before you decide that you are such a person, ask yourself a few questions:

1.   If you live in an area which is not well served by public transport, would it be possible for you to travel to work by

train if someone else were to take you to the station? Even if you had to take a taxi, it could well be that the aggravation you would save yourself would make the fare more than worthwhile. In addition, you would then be free to make use of the time spent travelling by making notes, preparing for meetings and so on, should you wish to do so.

2. If you have to make frequent use of your car during the day, are the journeys you would make local short-distance ones where some form of public transport could be used? Even if the public transport is not very reliable, it is worth considering whether the time (and, of course, the stress) saved by not having to look for parking spaces, plus the cost of parking – not to mention the petrol and the wear and tear on your vehicle – makes the use of a taxi worthwhile.

If you have considered both these possibilities and yet you still come to the conclusion that it is essential for you to have your own car at work, perhaps you should ask yourself a further question. If there are some days when you are less likely to use your car than others, would it be possible to share the journey with someone else who lives in your area? Not only would the stress of driving be yours on only half the number of days, the fact of having someone else to talk to often makes a journey far less traumatic than it would otherwise have been.

Let us suppose that, having looked at all the possibilities, it is still vitally important for you to drive yourself to work every day in your own car, what can you do to minimise the stress of that journey?

1. Would it be possible for you to change your hours of work slightly so that you were able to avoid the worst of the rush-hour traffic? There could be additional advantages at arriving at work early and leaving a little earlier than usual. You would have a relatively quiet time of day in which to do some work before the phones started to ring and people began to make demands upon your time. At the other end of the day you would have more time to

relax at home so that you did not remain on the
roundabout of work-sleep-work.

Of course you might be one of those who prefer to do
things the other way round and to arrive at work
somewhat later than usual and leave after the worst of the
rush-hour traffic. If you are someone who tends to go to
bed very late at night, then this would give you the chance
of sleeping a little later in the morning and therefore being
more refreshed. You would then have your 'quiet time' at
work at the end of the day rather than at the beginning.

2. At whatever time you travel, how do you spend the
time while driving? Observe yourself the next time you are
sitting in a traffic jam. Are your jaws tightly clenched? Are
you frowning? Are you drumming your fingers impatiently
on the steering wheel? Can you feel anger and impatience
surging within you? Are you only too conscious of the
heat, the dust, the fumes from a multitude of exhausts?
Stop! A combination of some or all of these feelings could
make you a prime candidate for some form of stress-
induced illness.

If it is absolutely essential that you spend a proportion of
your life sitting in your motor car on the way to or from
work, the very least you can do is try to ensure that the
journey is as pleasant as possible. If you know you are
going to have to travel during the rush-hour and that there
is nothing at all that you can do about it, what will fuming
and bad temper do except make you ill? If you have a radio
or a cassette player in your car, try to make the time pass
more pleasantly by listening to an interesting programme
or an enjoyable piece of music. If you are in a stationary
line of traffic, perhaps you can mentally prepare yourself
for the day's meetings. After all, if you are well prepared,
you are more liable to put your point clearly and
succinctly, and therefore the meeting will be shorter and
less stressful. If you find the tension of the traffic situation
increases when you try to think about business, perhaps
the answer is to indulge in some pleasant day-dreaming.

So you see there are many possible solutions to the traffic

problem. Even if none of the above apply, I have no doubt whatever that you are quite capable of finding a way of improving the situation if you would only set your mind to it.

Punctuality

If you are someone who is always late for appointments and meetings – or who never gets to work at the time you intend – you are causing yourself a great deal of unnecessary stress. (I am assuming that you are far too considerate a person to know that you are going to be late and not to care whether that is going to inconvenience others or upset anyone else's plans for the day.)

Sometimes, of course, the lateness is unavoidable – an emergency at home or the failure of the usual train to turn up at the station. In such cases, there is little or nothing you can do apart from informing other people. Even this is not always possible – there are not many communication channels open when sitting in an underground train in the middle of some dark tunnel, for example. Allowing yourself to get angry or impatient at the lateness does not make the train move any faster, or the hands of the clock any slower! All it does is to make your blood pressure go up and your temples throb, and cause you to become more and more stressed.

Most people who are in the habit of being late never *intend* to be. It is just that they leave everything to the last moment, or they do not make allowances for possible emergencies. Even a broken shoe lace can delay you long enough to make you miss your train if you had timed everything down to the last minute. The obvious answer, therefore, is to allow plenty of time, and even a little extra, for all that has to be done.

Those who unintentionally arrive late for appointments are always harassed and agitated by the time they arrive. This affects the way they speak and behave to others, and therefore naturally also affects the way others speak and behave towards them. It can often lead to ill-temper and obstinacy – hardly frames of mind which are most conducive to the successful outcome of a business meeting. In extreme cases it can even mean that, for the sake of a few extra minutes, terms can be unfavourable or deals can be lost altogether.

Yet what of the other extreme? Suppose you are someone who always gets everywhere far too early and then has to waste time hanging around for everyone else to turn up. You can either allow the situation to defeat you and make you angry with yourself for being so early (and of course when we are angry with ourselves it is not unusual to turn that anger outwards towards to other people) – or you can make use of the extra time which has fallen into your hands. You could spend some time preparing for a forthcoming meeting in even more detail than you had previously done. You could go for a short walk, have a cup of coffee or even practise one of the breathing exercises you will find in a later chapter. Any or all of those will calm and relax you, and therefore send you into the meeting in a better frame of mind and much more able to function efficiently.

Working Without a Break

If you never stop to take a break during the day – with the exception perhaps of a hastily munched sandwich at lunch-time – you are not only going to do yourself physical harm, you are actually going to achieve far less than you would if you worked for measured periods. It has actually been proved that the level of efficiency begins to drop after about 75 minutes of concentrated effort.

It is obviously not feasible to suggest that at the end of an hour and a quarter you get up and dash out of the meeting you are attending, or that you slam the phone down on a colleague and leave your desk. But do try to be realistic about the number of hours you work without a break (and I am referring to fairly intensified work, not to time which might be spent talking casually to others).

There are many different ways of having a break after an hour or two of concentrated effort. You do not have to go out for a walk – although actually this would do you the world of good and you should try to do it at least once a day, even if only for ten minutes or so. Sometimes all you need to do is get up from your desk and go and have a cup of tea or coffee. Perhaps you could just go into another room, sit in a comfortable chair and look at a newspaper for ten minutes.

Any or all of these things would provide an essential break from the pressure of work and, far from slowing down your pace and efficiency, you would find yourself working far better and far more effectively. Not only would you be having a mental rest from work, but you would also be releasing tension from your muscles – particularly those around your neck and shoulders – thereby reducing the possibility of developing a head or backache. Such physical discomfort would only make working even more difficult and would set you on that downward spiral of stress, pain and inefficiency.

Number of Hours Worked

Perhaps this section should have been headed 'the number of hours you are *seen* to work'? Within the companies for whom I have conducted workshops – and therefore probably within many others too – there seems to have grown up recently a belief that the more hours spent at your desk, the more efficient you will be. Or certainly that it is necessary to spend as many hours there as possible in order to convince your superiors that you are working harder (and therefore achieving more) than the next person.

Of course it does not follow that the more hours you put in the more you will achieve, particularly if those hours are worked without the type of breaks mentioned earlier. Indeed, in many cases the reverse is true. The more hours you put in over and above those which are essential, the more fatigued you will probably become and therefore the less efficient you are likely to be. Thus, any favourable impression you may have made upon others by your displays of zeal and diligence will be short-lived when actual results are noted.

It is obvious that if you work until you are exhausted, you are far more likely to make mistakes, and thus it is quite probable that valuable working time will have to be spent the following day correcting these errors. This, in turn, leads to more pressure upon the individual and in consequence even more stress. So not only would you not actually achieve more by working for longer than you are physically and mentally fit to do, you would in fact achieve far less, while at the same time increasing the risk of suffering from some sort of stress-induced illness.

Treatment of Employees

The man or woman who feels that they can only get results from their employees or subordinates by being aggressive and dictatorial is actually giving very clear indications of his or her own feelings of insecurity. This does not mean that you cannot be firm and in control of the situation as befits someone in a position of authority. But to be hurtful and sarcastic or to indulge in a display of bad temper is not only unworthy, it is also totally unproductive.

Suppose you have an employee who has either made an error or failed to complete some task required of him. If the person is by nature timid or shy and you act towards him in an angry and aggressive manner, what is likely to be the result? He will become even more nervous, and therefore even more liable to make mistakes or to be unable to work well.

If, however, the employee you have to deal with is made of stouter stuff – what happens then? You shout: he shouts back: you both lose control of your tempers and nothing is achieved except that two people become extremely stressed and agitated.

Of course you must put your point, you must state clearly what you expect of any individual and you must point out to others if they have made errors either of commission or omission. But protect both your business and your blood pressure by learning to do it in a firm and fair way. It is far better for all concerned if you are assertive rather than aggressive.

It is also a true but often forgotten fact that you will get a far better response from others if you *ask* them to do something than if you *tell* them to do it. Suppose you have a report that you would dearly like to have typed and ready by tomorrow morning. It is now four thirty and your secretary is due to finish for the day at five o'clock. Which of these approaches do you think is more likely to achieve the desired result?

> '*Miss Brown, have this report typed and on my desk by nine o'clock in the morning.*'

> '*Oh, Miss Brown, I realise that you are due to leave in half an hour but I wonder if you could help me. This report is very urgent and I really need to have it first thing in the morning. I wonder if you could possibly stay a little late and finish typing it for me; or perhaps you could come in a little earlier in the morning so that I can have it for the meeting at nine o'clock. I'm sorry to spring this on you at the last moment but I really would appreciate your help.*'

Miss Brown, faced with the first approach, is likely to think to herself, 'Who does he think he is? My day ends at five o'clock and at five o'clock I shall leave'. Yet Miss Brown, like all of us, likes to feel needed and important and when hearing approach number two is far more likely to think, 'He really does need my assistance so I'll do what I can to help him'.

Meetings

Many people, however senior their position, are nervous when faced with the prospect of meetings or presentations. This is only human nature. Indeed, some of our most famous actors – people who are used to appearing in public night after night – still suffer from nervousness before every performance. However, since meetings and presentations are usually vitally important so far as business is concerned, it is worth considering your approach to them.

If you do feel apprehensive at the thought of a forthcoming meeting, there are a few steps you can take to help yourself:

1.   Make sure you are well prepared. This may sound like an obvious statement but unless you have all the facts and figures at your fingertips, you are not going to feel at ease during the meeting itself. Although it is not possible to know in advance *every* question which is going to be raised, it is usually possible to anticipate the majority of them. So, when making your notes and preparing yourself for the meeting, spend some time considering what difficulties, if any, you are likely to encounter and how you can best overcome them.

2.   Don't leave things until the last moment. If you have to catch the 8.45 train in the morning, you will only agitate yourself if you start to collect your papers together at 8.30 a.m. You want to be in the calmest frame of mind possible, so ensure that everything you will need is assembled well in advance.

3.   If possible, arrive at your destination early and spend a few moments practising some breathing exercises (see Chapter Four). This only needs to take five minutes and can be done without anyone else realising what you are doing; yet the beneficial effects are enormous.

4.   If you are really anxious, it helps to spend some time the night before the meeting visualising the whole situation in your mind. See the scene in the board room as it will be in reality. Imagine yourself giving your report or presentation in a calm and clear manner, and then dealing with any questions which may arise in the same way. 'See' the expressions of approval on the faces of the others present. Such sessions of visualisation are extremely effective. After all, actors rehearse and rehearse so that they will perform perfectly on the night. All that you are doing is rehearsing a 'performance' in your mind.

5.   Remember that the others present are only human, each with their own fears and anxieties. You are not meeting with a collection of super-beings – even though there may be those who would like to think of themselves in that way. You are dealing with ordinary men and women, each of whom wants to do the very best for his or her company, and almost all of whom will be civil and

polite. If you should happen to encounter the 'business blusterer', remember that such behaviour is only a cover-up for feelings of self-doubt and insecurity, and you should pity him rather than allow him to disturb you in any way.

Now that you have considered some of the most stressful aspects of business and, hopefully, have made some changes in your own life, let us deal with how you cope with the tasks of each day.

The first suggestion may sound obvious: *clear your desk*. No one can work efficiently when surrounded by muddle and disorder. Try to have in front of you only what you need to accomplish each particular task, plus a notepad for anything which may arise which does not specifically concern the job in hand.

Planning is vital, and there is a lot to be said for lists! Take the time at regular intervals (once a day or once a week, depending on the type of business in which you are involved) to stop and plan precisely what you hope to accomplish in the coming period. Divide the tasks ahead into those things which urgently need to be done and those which you would like to do. There is no point in trying to set yourself impossible goals. You will only fail to reach them and this will cause you to think of yourself as a failure and will add to the stress in your life. Having divided the tasks in this way, list them in order of importance as indicated in the sample list below:

Must be done	Order of importance	Would like to do	Order of importance

Having decided on the task which is most important to you, take a good look at it and decide how you are going to handle it. How much time is it likely to take to complete? Remember to allow for interruptions; the telephone is bound to ring, and people around you are almost certain to have queries which need to be dealt with. Allow too for breaks for yourself so that you are able to work as efficiently as possible. Ask yourself whether any or all of this particular task can be delegated to others. Is there any part of it which is unnecessary and would therefore involve a waste of time and effort? Don't forget that you have to eat during the course of the day (or you certainly do if you wish to retain a sufficiently high energy level to perform efficiently). Take the time to check before commencing the task that you have all the relevant documentation.

Below is a sample of a checklist (similar to those used in many large organisations) which has proved its usefulness over the years:

Task	
Completion date	
Can I delegate?	

Time needed to complete	
Documents etc. needed	

Once you have dealt with all those tasks and actions which are essential, you can go on to deal with those you would like to do. If it is absolutely impossible to deal with each and every one of them, you will have to make some changes. In many cases this brings us straight back to the idea of delegation. You may feel that you would prefer to deal with everything yourself, but surely it is better for someone else to deal with it rather than to leave the task undone.

No one can achieve the impossible, so make sure that the targets you set yourself in terms of work to be accomplished are realistic. After all, if you were to collapse under the strain of overwork, nothing would be done at all.

Learn to say 'no' when necessary. This does not have to be done in an unpleasant or belligerent way. You can be perfectly polite while at the same time making sure that you do not feel compelled to undertake more than you can possibly achieve.

If the making of all these charts seems tedious to you, follow the example of many American executives: make one of each and merely photocopy them in any quantity you desire so that you then have a constant supply of them.

Once you have completed your charts or lists, check each night and see what you need to do on the following day. Make sure that you have access to all the information you might need, or at least that you know where to obtain it.

Checklist

Lifestyle Changes – Business

1. Delegate work where possible.

2. Try to travel early or late to avoid the worst of the traffic. Make use of travelling time – either to make plans or to relax, listen to music and so on.

3. Be punctual. Allow yourself plenty of time. If you are early, use the time to relax, practise breathing exercises and the like.

4. Take breaks while working. Get up from your desk. Get some fresh air if possible.

5. Work the number of hours necessary. Remember that more can be achieved in a shorter time if you are not tense and anxious.

6. Treat employees, subordinates and colleagues courteously. Ask for something rather than issuing commands.

7. Prepare adequately for meetings.

8. Make lists of those jobs which have to be done, making your priorities clear.

9. Don't make yourself ill by trying to achieve the impossible. Delegate where necessary.

Making Changes in your Home Life

Make time for the people in your life. If you have a husband
or wife and a family, remember that they do not want just a
money-earning machine. They want a real, live person who
cares about them and for whom they can care. The same
applies if you are unmarried, whether it is your parents, your
friends or your relatives. It is only too easy for partners to get
out of the habit of talking, and listening, to each other and
this can lead to innumerable problems, causing stress to each
partner and to the relationship as a whole.

Finding time to be together is of vital importance if a
relationship is to survive. So is finding time to be with your
children if they are not to grow up to be strangers to you. If
you allow your private life to become stressed, this fact is
bound to be reflected in your business life. The reverse is also
true. However pressurised and difficult your day has been, if
you carry that tension over into your home life, you will
cause difficulties there too. This does not mean that you
cannot talk about your problems at work – there is more than
a grain of truth in the old saying, 'A trouble shared is a
trouble halved' – for, even though your partner may not be
able to solve the problem for you, quite often somebody
looking at it from the outside can help to put the whole thing
in perspective. But remember that a true partnership works
both ways, and you must be prepared to listen to the other
person's problems too.

Just as it is important to find time to be with the people you
care for, it is also vital for everyone to find time to be alone.
Each individual deserves some privacy, yet all too often we
are made to feel guilty for wanting to be by ourselves. To
avoid any misunderstanding, explain to others that you need
some time to 'unwind', to be yourself, and that this does not
mean that you do not care for their company. Although you
must be prepared to allow them to do the same should they
wish it.

Many people, if they think of relaxation, think of hobbies.
Indeed, indulging in a hobby is an excellent way of
'switching off' the cares of the day. However, so many men
and women come home after what is essentially a competi-

tive day in the world of business, only to indulge in some competitive hobby such as squash, golf, or tennis. I am in no way decrying any of these activities – they are all excellent – but the element of competitiveness involved creates its own stresses. Think about your own hobbies and pastimes. Do they all have an element of competition in them? If so, you could be substituting one form of stress for another. You do not have to give up these competitive hobbies, but you should also try to find at least one which does not contain that element. Whether you like to read, to work in the garden, to go for long walks, to listen to music or to paint pictures – any of these would be an excellent antidote to the stress of business life.

It is very tempting, as financial recompense increases, to desire a bigger and more beautiful home, a newer and more powerful car and all the material trappings of wealth. This is fine, so long as you do not over-reach yourself. Your home should be a pleasure and a delight, not a source of anxiety. Financial worries account for a large number of stress-related illnesses, particularly strokes and heart attacks. What value is there in the most beautiful home and the largest car in the district if you are so ill that you are unable to enjoy them?

'I haven't had time for a holiday for seven years' – this is the proud boast of more than one executive who considers himself absolutely indispensable to the company. If that same executive were to suffer a massive stroke and be completely incapacitated, one would soon see just how well things went on without him! A holiday – whether or not it involves a change of environment – is essential to the well-being of each individual. It is a time when he can relax away from the pressures of work, a time when he can be together with the family and indulge in his hobbies. A change of scene is often to be desired, partly because of the interest and pleasure it can generate, and partly because it means that you are not at the other end of the telephone! So take the time for a complete break every now and then to counteract the stress of your usual life.

If it is good for you to relax and eat properly during business hours, it is even more vital that you sit and enjoy your meals at home. A mealtime is more than an opportunity to absorb the required vitamins and minerals and to put an end to pangs of hunger. It is a time for enjoying conversation, for being together with other people, for relaxing and providing a complete contrast to the working day. So make an occasion of mealtimes; ensure that they are something to look forward to, that they enhance your home life and the time you share with those you care for.

While on the subject of meals, are you one of those who dashes out of the house in the morning having had no breakfast, or perhaps having gobbled a piece of toast while rushing from room to room packing papers into your briefcase? Getting up half an hour earlier may not sound as if it is the answer to stress in your life – but give it a try. Just for a couple of weeks try getting up half an hour earlier every working day. This will give you time to slow down, to have breakfast, to talk to your family and to make sure that you have everything you need for the day. It can ensure that you start off in a completely unstressed frame of mind, and this can set the pattern for your entire day.

Make time for your friends and relatives. There is nothing in life more important than people. The poorest people in the world are those with a great deal of money – and no friends.

Is yours a household where bills never get paid until the red demand comes through the letter box? To some people this seems clever, but any form of financial pressure can only be bad for you. You would ease a great deal of the stress from your life if you were able to ensure that all financial matters were dealt with promptly and efficiently (and I am not in the employ of the Water Board!). Decide who in your own household is to be in charge of dealing with such things as mortgage payments, settlement of household bills and so on, and then let them be dealt with regularly as a matter of course. You can rush out and pay for each service just before the men arrive to cut it off, but the toll on your peace of mind will be far greater than the pleasure you will get from earning a few pennies in interest by delaying payment.

Homes which are so perfect that no one dares to sit on a chair for fear of disturbing the cushions are the most uncomfortable places to live in. On the other hand, homes which are in a complete clutter are also uncomfortable to the mind of the individual and can actually cause more tension than might be anticipated. Whether you live alone or in a crowded household, try to ensure that there is a certain amount of order in your environment. Apart from the fact that you will feel better about yourself and your surroundings, you are less likely to lose that vital piece of paper when you most need it!

Checklist

Lifestyle Changes – Home

1. Develop and enjoy relationship with those closest to you. Talk to them – and listen to them.
2. Take time to be alone when you feel you need it, without feeling guilty.
3. Make sure that at least one of your hobbies is non-competitive.
4. Do not over-reach yourself financially.
5. Take breaks and holidays whenever possible.
6. Make an occasion out of mealtimes.
7. Get up half and hour earlier to allow yourself a relaxed start to the day.
8. Remember to make time for your friends and relatives.
9. Ensure that household finances are dealt with promptly.
10. Try to avoid living in a clutter.

You now have a comprehensive list of ways – some of them seemingly small and insignificant – in which you can change your lifestyle. Some of them may already be part of your life; or you may feel that some of them do not apply to you. But all of them are possible. And all of them will reduce the amount of stress in your life. There are bound to be stressful factors and events which are unavoidable, so let us at least eliminate those which do not have to exist.

It may not be possible to make all these changes in one fell swoop, but there is no reason why you cannot begin with one or two of them – and begin *today*! Once you have proved to yourself that they work and that you do have less stress in your life, you can go on to put the others into practice one by one.

CHAPTER FOUR

Stress-Proof Yourself
– Starting Now!

The methods of releasing tension from the mind and body are many and various: massage, Alexander technique, hypnosis, and aromatherapy are just a few which are becoming more and more readily available. Excellent as all these techniques are, perhaps the simplest and most effective form is the one which you can practise for yourself, in your own home and in your own time: learning to relax.

You may be thinking to yourself that this may not be possible for you to achieve, that you are one of those people who can 'never relax'. There is no such person. Relaxation, like anything else worthwhile, can be learned. What could be more worthwhile than a simple process requiring no complicated equipment, which can not only improve the quality of your life, but could even save it?

In this chapter you will find several different relaxation techniques. Practise each one (not just once, but over a period of at least three weeks) and see which suits you the best. All it takes is fifteen minutes or so of your time twice a day – isn't it worth a try? Learn to make relaxation a habit, just like cleaning your teeth. Let it become a part of your daily routine. The ideal times for practising are first thing in the morning (yes, you *do* have the time, even if it means getting up fifteen minutes earlier), and at the end of the day – perhaps when you arrive home from work so that you are able to 'turn off' the pressures of business and start your evening in a calm and stress-free state of mind.

Relaxation does not mean just sitting in a chair and doing

nothing, or staring at a television screen. At times like that you are still likely to have all sorts of problems and worries racing around in your head. Nor is sleeping the same thing as relaxing – although it does have its part to play – as sleep can be either calm or troubled. Once you have found the method of relaxation which is most suitable for you and have practised it regularly, you will find that you are able to enter a temporary state of inner calm at will, far away from the pressures of your everyday life.

Interesting and beneficial physiological changes take place when you are relaxed:

- your blood pressure is immediately lowered;

- your heart beat slows;

- muscle tension decreases;

- your body's demand for oxygen is lessened;

- the flow of blood to your organs and muscles decreases;

- your natural output of cortisone is reduced.

The combination of the changes listed above will make an immediate difference to the way you feel. Your sense of well-being will immediately increase. You will also think more clearly and will therefore be more efficient in all that you do. Thus, you will more than make up for the fifteen minutes you may have spent practising your relaxation exercise first thing in the morning.

Breathing

It is usually supposed that our energy comes from the food that we eat – and to a certain extent it does. However, without the oxygen from the air we breathe the body could not break down the nutrients contained in that food in order to produce energy.

Correct breathing and a sufficient intake of air affects your looks, your health, your vitality and your ability to think clearly. With all these benefits waiting for you, surely it is worth spending a little time learning to breathe properly and practising an exercise or two.

Breathing in supplies the body with oxygen and breathing out eliminates carbon dioxide and wastes from the system. If that carbon dioxide is not removed, your cells will become contaminated and will eventually die. Most people only use fifty per cent of their breathing potential which means that they are only absorbing fifty per cent of oxygen and, worse still, only eliminating fifty per cent of those potentially poisonous wastes. This in turn means that less oxygen is available to supply the blood, the nerves, the skin and the brain. It is widely believed that lack of oxygen to the brain can prematurely precipitate those conditions which were previously associated only with old age such as senility, lack of memory and vagueness of mind. Many therapists, particularly in the United States, have achieved great success in the treatment of chest complaints, fatigue and depression simply by teaching their patients to breathe correctly.

The link between breathing and emotions is easier to see for yourself. When someone gets into a panic, their breathing becomes shallow and rapid, which in turn affects the clarity of their thinking. You can try the reverse of this process for yourself. Next time you feel tense or upset, force yourself to breathe slowly and regularly and you will actually become aware that you are gaining more and more control over the situation.

The following are a few breathing exercises for you to try. I would suggest that you work on these for a week or two before going on to practise the actual relaxation exercises which follow. Experiment by practising each exercise for a few days so that you will know which one is most suitable for you. I think you will be surprised both at how shallow your breathing has been in the past and at how much better you will feel once you have learned to breathe properly. Also, of course, once you have mastered the technique of breathing correctly in order to release tension, this is something which can quite easily and unnoticeably be practised while sitting on a train or in an aeroplane.

Exercise 1

Lie on the floor or on a bed without pillows. Place your hands on your ribcage so that your fingertips are just touching. Breathe in using your chest and your abdomen. Make sure that you can feel your diaphragm expanding so that your fingertips are forced apart. Most people only breathe with the upper part of the body which means that they are not fully expanding their lungs or taking in sufficient oxygen. As you breathe out try and release just as much air as you took in. Continue for about five minutes and practise at least twice a day until you find that you are breathing deeply and that your fingertips are forced apart without you having to make a concentrated effort to ensure that this is so.

Exercise 2

This exercise is useful whenever your head feels stuffy or when you are feeling particularly tense.

Stand with your feet slightly apart, your hands on your ribs. Breathe in *slowly* through the nose for a count of ten. Feel your ribcage expanding and try to avoid the tendency to raise your shoulders. Hold your breath for a *slow* count of three. Breathe out for a count of ten making sure that you expel all the air you have taken in. Repeat three times.

Exercise 3

Stand with your feet slightly apart and your arms loosely by your sides. Breathe in deeply through your nose. Stand on tiptoe and tense your body as much as possible – clench your fists, raise your shoulders and tighten your jaw muscles. Lower your heels to the ground and then, as you slowly breathe out through your mouth, release all the tension from your body. Make sure that your jaw is relaxed, that your shoulders are lowered and that your arms are loosely by your sides again. Repeat four times. This exercise is excellent for an instant release of tension.

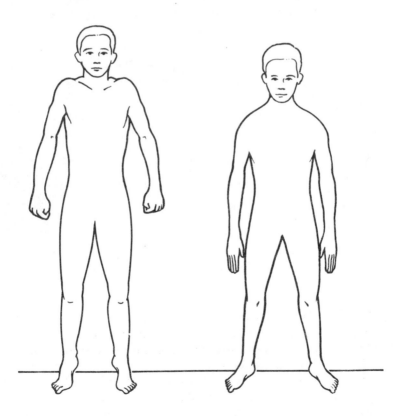

Relaxation

The following exercises are intended to relax the body, although in fact the mind, body and emotions are so interdependent that it is impossible to separate them. No one is trying to suggest that relaxation itself can solve your problems or make your decisions for you. What it can do, however, is change your reactions to what is going on around you, thereby improving your physical health and your mental state, and reducing your susceptibility to stress-related illnesses.

You may not find these relaxation techniques easy when you first try them but I do urge you to persevere. You might find it helpful if someone reads the instructions out to you, or perhaps you could record them onto a cassette and play it back to yourself as you practise. Of course it is also now possible to buy pre-recorded relaxation cassettes which could assist you.

If you are unused to relaxing you may well find that your mind has a tendency to wander from what you should be doing and that distractive thoughts creep in from time to time. Don't worry – that is quite normal. The most important thing is not to let it put you off what you are doing. Allow these thoughts into your mind, tell yourself that you will deal with them later, and then gently let them go. Don't try to *force* them out, and don't get annoyed with yourself for allowing them to enter in the first place; you will merely destroy all that you are aiming for.

Exercise 1

This is a basic relaxation technique and, like any other, should be practised twice a day for about three weeks to determine whether it is the most suitable exercise for you.

Lie on your bed or sit in a comfortable chair, preferably one which has a high enough back to support your head and neck. Close your eyes.

Tense the muscles of your feet as much as you can without actually hurting yourself. Then, all at once, let the tension go and relax your feet. Now do the same with your legs and your thighs.

Now clench your fists as tightly as possible and feel the tension spreading up your arms to your shoulders. Hold that position for a few moments before releasing the tension all in one go.

Let the whole of the trunk of your body become tense and rigid and become aware of what that rigidity feels like before you relax and let your body become loose and heavy as you sit in your chair or lie on your bed.

Now concentrate on the area where the greatest tension arises – your head (particularly around the jaw), your neck and your shoulders. Feel the tension there; be aware that your jaw is tightening, let your shoulders come up towards your ears, frown, clench your teeth. Then release all that tension in one fell swoop so that your shoulders become heavy, your jaw relaxes and all the frown lines disappear from your face.

Now, having dispersed all that physical tension from your body, just remain where you are and concentrate on your breathing. Breath slowly and evenly for a few minutes – in through the nose and out through the mouth. Establish an even rhythm of breathing and really feel, as you exhale, that you are breathing out all the accumulated tension from your body.

The most difficult part of this, or any relaxation exercise, is to do it *slowly*. There is a great temptation to rush the whole process, but if you allow yourself to give in to this temptation you will in fact be defeating the whole object. So take your time. You will find, even when you are doing it slowly, that the whole thing will take no more than fifteen minutes from start to finish. (If it takes you much less time than that, you are doing it far too quickly.)

Exercise 2

For this exercise you need to sit on the floor, on a stool or on the side of your bed – somewhere where you do not have a support for your back.

Place your hands on your hips. Close your eyes.

Bending your upper body forwards, then to the right, then leaning backwards and then to the left, make a large circle with your body.

Continue moving in the same way making the circles smaller and smaller until you are hardly moving at all and then finally stop.

Once you are quite still, concentrate on your breathing. Breathe slowly, counting 'one' silently in your head each time that you breathe in and 'two' each time that you breathe out. Make sure that you breathe deeply in order to absorb as much oxygen as possible.

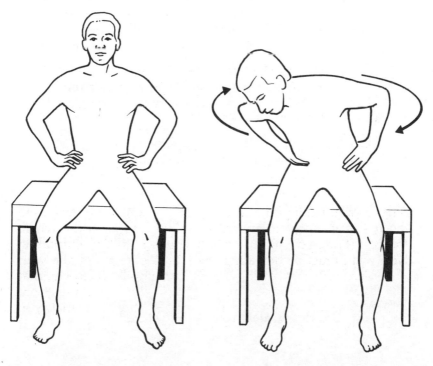

Exercise 3

> Lie on your bed or on the floor. Close your eyes and
> breathe slowly and regularly.
>
> Concentrate on your feet and use your imagination
> to convince you that your feet are growing heavier
> and heavier. Then, still using your imagination, make
> that heaviness creep up your legs and thighs to your
> hips. When you feel that they do indeed feel heavy,
> lie there for a few moments and allow yourself to be
> fully aware of the sensation.
>
> Now do precisely the same thing with your hands
> and your arms. Imagine them growing heavier and
> heavier until you can really feel the weight of them.
>
> Next, use your imagination to make your body
> itself become heavy as you lie on the floor or on your
> bed. Try to be aware of your muscles relaxing.
>
> Let that heaviness travel upwards to your shoul-
> ders, so that they press down upon the surface
> beneath you. As your jaw grows heavier, feel your
> mouth come open a little. Make sure that your head
> itself is heavy too, imagine that it would just be too
> much of an effort to raise it.
>
> Now imagine that your eyelids are so heavy that it
> would be too great an effort to try and open your
> eyes.
>
> Once you feel that heaviness overwhelm your body
> from feet to head, lie still and concentrate on deep,
> even breathing.

This is not the easiest of exercises for anyone unused to
relaxation but it is well worth persevering with as the
benefits from it are considerable. It may well be that when
you first try it, it takes several minutes just to imagine that
your feet are becoming heavy. If this is so, don't let it worry
you as you will achieve the desired result in the end. It is,
however, a very good indication that you are one of those
people who is desperately in need of relaxation.

Exercise 4

This is really a basic yoga technique. It stretches your body and also increases your awareness, giving you more energy and capacity for work and play.

Stand easily with your hands at your sides. Make sure that your hands are relaxed and your fists are not clenched.

Inhale slowly, turning your hands at the same time so that your palms face upwards. As you continue to breathe in, raise your arms so that your palms come together above your head.

Keeping your arms in that position, breathe out and rise up on to your toes.

Still in the same position, breathe in and hold your breath for a count of five.

Slowly exhale, coming down from your toes and bringing your arms slowly back to the starting position.

Exercise 5

This exercise, which is primarily for the head and shoulders, is particularly beneficial when you have spent some time sitting at your desk or driving your car.

Sitting in a straight–backed chair with your spine straight, drop your head forward so that your chin touches your chest.

Circle your head – to the right, then dropping it backwards and then to the left – three times. Repeat in the opposite direction.

Now rotate your right shoulder, bringing it up towards your ear, then forwards, lowering it and then bring it backwards. Do this twice and then repeat in the other direction.

Repeat the process with your left shoulder.

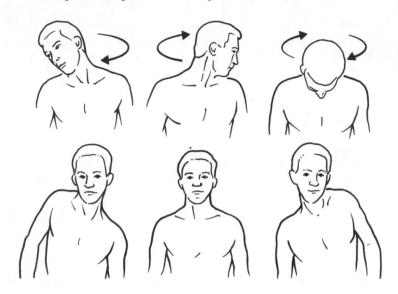

Exercise 6

This is an exercise for your eyes and is an excellent one to use after time spent concentrating on documents, staring at the screen of a VDU or driving in bright sunlight.

Keeping your head still and staring straight ahead of you, exercise your eye muscles by looking up and down, then to the left and to the right. Repeat twice.

Hold a pencil at arm's length. Focus upon it and then let your vision go beyond the pencil to the furthest extremity of the room. Now bring your gaze back again until the pencil is clearly in focus. Repeat twice.

Close your eyes and imagine that your eyelids are growing heavier and heavier. Remain in that position for a few moments.

Exercise 7

This final exercise is one for total relaxation combined with correct alignment of the spine. You may find it slightly uncomfortable at first but you will benefit greatly if you persevere with it.

Lie on your back on the floor. Rest your head on a pile of about four paperback books (normal size, not the extremely thick ones). Have the soles of your feet flat on the floor and your knees raised in a comfortable position. Place your hands gently on your ribcage.

Close your eyes and spend a few moments concentrating on deep and even breathing.

Now picture a scene in your mind – one which gives you pleasure and which you find relaxing. It can be a scene which you remember from the past, one which you know well now or even one created totally in your imagination. The important thing is that you find the whole process calming and pleasurable.

Once you have chosen your image, examine it in detail. If you have decided upon a seascape, note the weather, the colours of the sky and the sea. Are there any boats around? Or perhaps some seabirds? Spend at least ten minutes getting to know the image you have chosen and seeing it from every viewpoint.

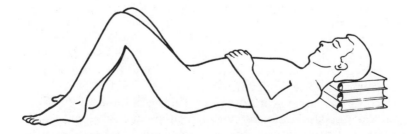

Sleep

Sleep is a very valuable and therapeutic state. It is a natural healer, regenerating both the mind and the body. And yet, when you are stressed, it is the one thing which is often the most difficult to achieve.

You know what it is like. You go to bed with your mind full of the problems from the day which has just passed and the worries concerning the day which is yet to come. You may be tired and yet you lie there for hour upon hour, tossing and turning, trying desperately to go to sleep and knowing that if you fail, you will be even less able to cope with the problems of work and home when tomorrow comes. Somehow the more you try to sleep, the more sleep evades you. When you finally drop off, it seems like only minutes before the ringing of the alarm clock wakens you to face another day.

Does all that sound familiar? Have you ever felt yourself trapped on that merry-go-round of lack of sleep and mental and physical exhaustion? Then now is the time to do something about it.

First of all, don't worry if you do not sleep for the 'correct' eight hours a night. You may in fact be one of those people who only needs five or six hours sleep, just as others may need nine or even ten. There is no hard and fast rule concerning the amount of sleep one should have – provided that sleep, when it comes, is deep and untroubled. You are hardly likely to be relaxed and untroubled if you lie there watching the hands of the clock and worrying that there are only six hours left before it is time to get up.

Remember too that, while a baby may seem almost to sleep around the clock, we all need less and less sleep as we get older. It is not unusual for people in their seventies to require no more than five hours sleep a night. If you can go to sleep quite easily, if that sleep is deep and sound and if you wake refreshed and ready to face the coming day, then the number of hours is totally irrelevant.

Do not be anxious if you have the occasional night when you do not sleep as you would have wished. That is not unusual. The only time to be concerned is when you *never* seem to get a good night's sleep. In addition, don't worry if you find it difficult to get up in the morning even though you feel you have slept well. Take note of how you feel after being up for about ten minutes. If you feel bright and alert then your sleep was sufficient but if you feel slow and thick-headed then either you need more hours of sleep or the quality of the sleep you are getting is poor.

A great deal of insomnia is caused because the sufferer builds on past failures. Perhaps John Smith goes to bed the night before an important meeting and, for some reason, is unable to sleep. He is worried about the coming day and is anxious to get as much sleep as possible – but none comes. The following night when he goes to bed he thinks to himself, 'I am *so* tired – I really must get some sleep tonight'. If he does not fall asleep almost instantly, he begins to worry; 'I couldn't bear another night like last night. I really *must* get some sleep'. But of course, the harder he tries, the less likely he is to sleep, and then he has two failures to build upon instead of one.

So it goes on. Each night John Smith grows more and more desperate. Each night he tries harder and harder to sleep – and to no avail. Eventually the time comes when he can say, 'I haven't slept for over a week' (although of course if this were factual, he would be more than a little unwell; what he is really saying is that his sleep has been broken and troubled). Soon he has built up a picture of himself as an insomniac whereas in reality, he is just a man who had trouble sleeping on one occasion.

It is possible that vitamin or mineral deficiencies can lead to sleep problems. It may be necessary to check your diet. You will find more about this subject in the next chapter.

The following are some simple ways of helping yourself to break the pattern of sleepless nights which may have developed:

1.   Don't go to bed if you still feel wide awake. Read a book or magazine for pleasure or listen to some music. This is *not* the time to do that little bit of extra work or you will merely drive sleep further and further away from you. Whatever you decide to do should be enjoyable and relaxing.

2.   Be certain that you get some physical exercise during the course of each day – even if it is just brisk walking – but try to ensure that it is not just prior to bedtime as you will have quickened your heartbeat and your pulse rate, and this is the opposite of the effect you wish to achieve.

3.   Try not to drink tea or coffee too late in the evening. The caffeine they contain is a stimulant and could well keep you awake. If you drink decaffeinated coffee, do check that it is one of those which tells you on the label that it has been 'naturally decaffeinated' as the chemicals used to remove the caffeine from some of the cheaper varieties can do you more harm than the caffeine itself.

4.   Avoid drinking alcohol too late in the evening. Even if it is tempting to have a nightcap, this is not necessarily a good idea if you tend to have difficulty sleeping. Although the alcohol in a late-night drink may well help you to go to sleep initially, it won't keep you asleep and you will be more likely to wake up several times during the night.

5.   It is far harder to sleep in a stuffy atmosphere, so don't smoke (or allow others to smoke) in the bedroom if you normally have any trouble sleeping. Quite apart from the harmful effects of smoking, you are likely to have difficulty in getting to sleep and also find that you wake up with a head which is far from clear.

6.   Have a bath just before going to bed, but make sure that it is lukewarm, as water which is either too hot or too cold is likely to act as a stimulant.

7.   There is a great deal to be said for establishing a pre-bedtime routine. By doing the same things each night prior to going to bed, you are forming a link in your subconscious mind between those actions and the fact that sleep will follow. So, whether you put out the milk bottles, the light or the cat, try to do things in the same order each night.

8.   The beneficial effect of a drink of warm milk before bedtime is not just an old wives' tale; it will in fact help you to relax and therefore probably to sleep. Or you could try a drink of camomile tea. Camomile tea is now easily

available in health shops as well as some supermarkets and can be bought in teabag form as well as loose. If you are not used to the taste you may prefer to sweeten it with a spoonful of honey.

9. Once you are in bed, practise the following mental relaxation exercise, remembering that problems are caused by people trying to *go* to sleep instead of relaxing and allowing sleep to *come* to them.

Close your eyes and take your mind on a walk in a place of your imagination. You may choose to stroll along a country lane, to make footprints on a sandy beach or to walk barefoot in a beautiful garden. The setting is not important as long as it is one which you find pleasant and relaxing. Of course it does not have to be the same one every night. Begin to walk in the place you have chosen, seeing your surroundings in as much detail as possible, and making sure that you have to turn corners or go round bends so that there is always more to see. If you are in a garden, the flowers will vary according to the season. If you are in a country lane, the fields and hedgerows will be filled with different colours at different times of the year. The world is yours; you can visit in your mind a place that you know well or one that you vaguely remember. You can invent a beauty spot or two of your own. The most important thing is to enjoy it, and to know that you will never reach the most distant part of that particular place – for you will have fallen asleep!

CHAPTER FIVE

You Are What You Eat

There are many areas in your life over which you may have little or no control. You cannot always dictate the amount of business you are asked to handle in any specific period; you may not be able to avoid travelling in order to deal with that business; you are not responsible for the idleness or inefficiency of others; it is not your fault if an essential document is lost in the post. One of the things over which you have total control, however, is what you put into your body in the form of food and drink.

Now this is not a chapter advocating the imposition of an impossibly strict regime of self-denial. Indeed, forcing yourself to adhere to a drastic series of dietary rules which are dramatically different to any you have formerly known would only add to your problems. The stress that results from feelings of deprivation when you are denied your favourite foods would do you more harm than good. What is being suggested here is that you try first of all to observe your general diet, and to become aware of any areas where it could be improved. Then you can attempt to improve it in such a way that it interferes as little as possible with what you would *choose* to eat and drink were there no health considerations to take into account.

It is an accepted fact that someone whose diet is basically healthy and provides all the vitamins and minerals they need is much more able to withstand the physical effects of stress. It is also a fact that in so-called 'civilised' countries, the majority of people are not having a diet which contains all the necessary elements of sound nutrition – proteins, vitamins and minerals. Is it a coincidence that it is in these countries that the level of stress is higher, as are the numbers of deaths from strokes and heart disease?

Even those people who think they have sufficient knowledge to ensure that they are getting a balanced diet are having their efforts thwarted by modern agricultural processes. Over-cropping of the land and the extensive use of chemical fertilisers means that the soil has become deficient in vital elements. This, of course, means that the crops raised on that soil are deficient in just the same way. In addition, all foods have their highest nutritional value when they have just been gathered so, by the time they have travelled from the farmer through the transporters, the processors, the packers to the supermarket store-room and then onto the shelves and eventually to the consumer – to you – a great deal of that nutritional value will have been destroyed.

So, although it may not always be practicable, you will in fact be helping your health if you can buy fresh foods locally and as you need them rather than, as is common in many families these days, making one massive shopping expedition every week or two.

It is often very difficult for any individual to assess whether or not he is suffering from a vitamin or mineral deficiency but as a general guide the following are the most common visible symptoms. If any or all of them apply to you then you are in a high risk proportion of the population and, in addition to regulating your diet, you would do well to take some supplements in tablet form. The most common symptoms of deficiency are:

- dry, flaky skin;
- ridges or white flecks on the fingernails;
- very red tongue;
- dry skin at the corners of your mouth and around your nose;
- tendency to bleeding gums and mouth ulcers;
- dull, dry hair;

- low energy level;
- bruise easily;
- heal slowly.

Sugar

You probably already know that a high sugar consumption is bad for you as refined sugar provides a great many calories but contains no beneficial elements. An excessive sugar intake can cause you to suffer from low blood sugar (hypoglycaemia) which in turn can cause irritability and fatigue. For someone with a tendency to suffer from stress, this is the last thing you would want as it can only serve to increase the likelihood of suffering from a stress-related illness or disease.

Fats

Fat consumption is the major cause of heart disease, and heart disease is the biggest single killer in Britain today. In fact, in 1980 almost one third of all deaths from heart disease in England and Wales were men under 65. Therefore, it makes a great deal of sense to limit severely your intake of fat and fatty food, particularly if you are in a stressful occupation.

Salt

Too much salt causes high blood pressure and this in turn causes heart disease and strokes. In their book *The Food Scandal* (Century 1984), Caroline Walker and Geoffrey Cannon say:

Heart disease and stroke are major health problems in Western countries. In England and Wales in 1980 the number of deaths ascribed to high blood pressure was 6,893; to heart disease 160,458; and to stroke 73,532. This totals 240,883 – virtually a quarter of a million people a year. The total of deaths from these causes under the age of sixty-five was also very high: 47,028 – nearly fifty thousand people!

Surveys have been done in countries where there is known to be a low intake of salt in the diet. It has been found that there is no blood pressure problem at all among the populations of these countries. The reverse is also true, and in countries where there is a high intake of salt, the problem of high blood pressure is significant and on the increase.

Let us assume that, because you are a concerned and intelligent individual who does not particularly want to suffer from a stroke or a heart attack, you have decided to do something about your diet. Where do you start?

First of all, the changes do not have to be dramatic or drastic. You would be amazed at how small alterations in your cooking and eating habits can make a tremendous difference. Below you will find some hints for ways of altering your diet in such a way that the differences will be almost unnoticeable. It does not mean that you are no longer able to eat at restaurants or hotels; it does not mean that you have to become a fanatic who will never allow one 'forbidden' food to pass your lips. What we want is to change your basic routine. Nothing – even if it is on the list of foods to avoid – cannot be enjoyed on the odd occasion without doing you any undue harm. Although, once you have made the basic changes in your diet, you are quite likely to find that your desire for former 'treats' has greatly diminished.

Simple Changes You Can Make to Your Diet

Fats

Fry less, grill more.

Avoid putting butter on vegetables.
Spread butter, margarine or low-fat spread more thinly.

Meat and Poultry

Have smaller amounts of meat – ideally not more than 6 oz
a day.
Stick to the leaner cuts of meat.
Avoid red meat as much as possible.
Remove skin from poultry.
Grill instead of frying.
Cut off all visible fat.
Avoid meat pies.
Avoid tinned meat.

Fish

Eat more fresh fish.
Avoid fish in batter.
Avoid ready-prepared convenience meals of fish in fatty
sauce.

Cereals

Eat more wholegrain cereal.
Add honey or fresh fruit rather than sugar.
Eat more wholemeal or wholegrain bread.

Cakes and Biscuits

Eat less often – keep them for special occasions.
Choose the less sweet varieties (for example, teacakes or
scones).

Salt

Never add salt to the meal on your plate.
Avoid pre-packaged foods which have a very high salt
content.

Use as little as possible in cooking – try herbs, lemon juice etc.
If you must use salt, make sure that it is natural sea-salt.

Drinks

Acquire a taste for decaffeinated coffee and herb tea.
Only drink alcohol in moderation.
Drink spring water or filtered water as opposed to water from the tap.
Drink fruit juice instead of fruit squashes which are very high in colouring and preservatives.

Sugar Products

Buy 'low sugar' jams or honey instead of jams with a high sugar content.
If using tinned fruit, buy that which is canned in its own juice as opposed to one in a sugar syrup.

White Flour Products

Eat as little as possible of pastry, white bread, etc.
Substitute wholemeal products for those made with white flour.

Rice and Pasta

Substitute brown rice for white.
Choose wholemeal pasta instead of that made with white flour.

Get into the habit of reading labels so that you can avoid those foods which are very high in preservatives, colourings and harmful additives.

Learn to eat more slowly. Not only will you find that you enjoy your food more, you will aid your digestion and be more aware when you have actually had enough to eat.

Vitamins, Minerals and Trace Elements

Having a healthy body would not make it impossible for you to suffer from a stress-related illness, but it will certainly provide you with a measure of protection. A correct balance of vitamins, minerals and trace elements is essential if you want to have a healthy body.

The section which follows contains a list of the essentials for maintaining good health, indicates from which foods those essentials can be obtained and the role that they play. If you already have a balanced diet you will probably find that most of them are already included in your daily intake of food. But look down the list and see if there are any which appear to be missing from your normal diet. Perhaps there is a particular range of foods which you dislike, in which case you do not have to force yourself to eat them, but you can at least make up for this by taking the necessary vitamin or mineral in tablet form.

In addition, if you are suffering from a particular health problem, it would be as well to look at the list of symptoms to see if you can discover what vital element you may be lacking. This can then be added to your diet, either in the form of a food containing that element, or of a vitamin tablet.

VITAMIN A

Found in: green vegetables, liver, kidney, milk, cream, cheese.

Function: structure of skin and mucous membrane; necessary for correct growth; health of the eyes.

Symptoms of deficiency: catarrh, bronchial complaints; low resistance to infection; night blindness.

VITAMIN B1

Found in: green vegetables, milk, eggs, meat, liver, yeast, wheat germ.

Function: balanced metabolism; vital for growth; fitness of the heart; function of nerves and muscles.

Symptoms of deficiency: ulcers; nervous disorders, depression; blood disorders; problems of skin and hair.

VITAMIN B2

Found in: green vegetables, peanuts, milk, eggs, meat, poultry, yeast, wheat germ.

Function: general well-being; vital for growth, health of hair and mouth; function of eyes.

Symptoms of deficiency: nervous disorders; mouth and tongue sores; poor vision; dry hair and skin; lack of stamina.

VITAMIN B3

Found in: brown rice, bran, liver, yeast, eggs, all whole grain products.

Function: growth of all tissue; health of skin and hair.

Symptoms of deficiency: dry hair and skin.

VITAMIN B6

Found in: milk, yolk of egg, fish, yeast, wheat germ, melon, cabbage.

Function: protein metabolism; function of nerves and muscles; health of skin.

Symptoms of deficiency: nervous rashes, skin eruptions; insomnia; irritability, cramps in muscles.

VITAMIN B12

Found in: eggs, liver, meat, yeast, spinach, lettuce.

Function: protein metabolism; health of nerve tissue; healthy skin.

Symptoms of deficiency: anaemia; skin problems; lack of appetite; excessive tiredness.

BIOTIN

Found in: vegetables, nuts, liver, kidney.

Function: healthy skin; function of nerves and muscles.

Symptoms of deficiency: poor skin condition; constant tiredness.

CHOLINE

Found in: egg yolk, liver, dried yeast, kidney.

Function: essential for liver; prevents build-up of fatty acids.

Symptoms of deficiency: premature ageing; build-up of fatty acids in the body.

FOLIC ACID

Found in: green leafy vegetables, brewer's yeast, liver.

Function: correct formation of red blood cells.

Symptoms of deficiency: anaemia.

PABA (PARA-AMINOBENZOIC ACID)

Found in: liver, yeast, wheat germ, molasses.

Function: aids red blood cell formation.

Symptoms of deficiency: depression; constipation; fatigue; irritability.

INOSITOL

Found in: eggs, meat, liver, kidney, whole grain products.

Function: correct functioning of liver; prevents build-up of fatty acids.

Symptoms of deficiency: build-up of fatty acids in the body; premature ageing.

NIACIN

Found in: milk, liver, kidney, yeast, whole grain products.

Function: correct growth; health of skin; healthy intestines and nerves; correct functioning of stomach.

Symptoms of deficiency: skin disorders, nervous and intestinal disorders; insomnia, headaches.

VITAMIN C

Found in: citrus fruit, melon, tomatoes, raw vegetables, berries.

Function: vital for growth, cell activity; health of teeth and gums.

Symptoms of deficiency: sore gums; pains in joints; lack of immunity to infection.

VITAMIN D

Found in: milk, butter, fish, eggs, green vegetables.

Function: formation of bones and teeth; regulating calcium and phosphorus.

Symptoms of deficiency: tooth decay; bone deformity; calcium deficiency.

VITAMIN E

Found in: green vegetables, egg yolks, milk, seed germ oils.

Function: reproduction; correct function of nerves and muscles.

Symptoms of deficiency: incomplete pregnancies; sterility in males; premature ageing; muscular and nervous disorders.

VITAMIN F

Found in: soya, corn oil.

Function: regulates blood coagulation; vital for normal glandular activity.

Symptoms of deficiency: brittle hair and nails; varicose veins; dandruff.

VITAMIN K

Found in: green leafy vegetables, soya beans, vegetable oil, tomatoes, liver.

Function: blood clotting.

Symptoms of deficiency: prolonged bleeding from wounds.

COBALT

Found in: milk, liver, kidneys.

Function: maintenance of red blood cells.

Symptoms of deficiency: pernicious anaemia.

COPPER

Found in: green leafy vegetables, liver, whole grain.

Function: formation of red blood cells.

Symptoms of deficiency: skin sores; general weakness.

IODINE

Found in: plant and animal seafoods.

Function: function of thyroid gland; regulation of body metabolism.

Symptoms of deficiency: enlarged thyroid gland; loss of energy; dry skin and hair.

IRON

Found in: green leafy vegetables, liver, dried apricots, walnuts.

Function: production of haemoglobin; promotes growth.

Symptoms of deficiency: anaemia; constipation; weakness.

ZINC

Found in: brewer's yeast, wheat bran, wheat germ.

Function: aids healing process; production of male reproduction fluid; insulin synthesis.

Symptoms of deficiency: delayed sexual maturity; retarded growth.

CALCIUM

Found in: milk, dairy products, bone meal.

Function: helps blood clotting; vital for function of heart nerves and muscles; strong bones and teeth.

Symptoms of deficiency: brittle bones; soft bones; weak teeth; pains in back and legs.

CHLORINE

Found in: sea salt.

Function: production of digestive acids; balance of acidity/ alkalinity.

Symptoms of deficiency: poor digestion; loss of hair and teeth.

MAGNESIUM

Found in: green vegetables, apples, almonds, corn, soya beans.

Function: aids body to utilise fats, proteins and other nutrients.

Symptoms of deficiency: nervousness; trembling.

PHOSPHORUS

Found in: eggs, fish, poultry, meat, whole grain, nuts.

Function: (with calcium) builds strong teeth and bones.

Symptoms of deficiency: loss of weight; poor appetite.

POTASSIUM

Found in: green leafy vegetables, oranges, whole grain, skins of potatoes.

Function: controls activity of nerves, kidneys and heart muscles.

Symptoms of deficiency: heart and respiratory failure.

SODIUM

Found in: seafoods, sea salt, kelp, meat, beets.

Function: vital for correct functioning of nerves, muscles, blood and lymph system.

Symptoms of deficiency: loss of appetite; nausea; weak muscles.

SULPHUR

Found in: eggs, fish, nuts, meat, cabbage, Brussels sprouts.

Function: formation of body tissues.

Symptoms of deficiency: poor formation of body tissue.

Finally, there is a range of foods which are readily and easily available and which are particularly effective in combating stress. Try to include as many of these in your normal diet as possible.

- green leafy vegetables;
- fresh fruit;

- dried fruit;

- soya products;

- wheat germ;

- low fat dairy food – such as cottage cheese or low fat yoghurt.

Not only are these foods easy to obtain, they are excellent for those times during a hectic working day when there may not be sufficient time to enjoy a well-balanced meal. Cottage cheese followed by some fresh and dried fruit is easy to eat (even if there is no time to leave the office or if you are on the way to a meeting), easy to digest, and far better for you than a pie and a pint of beer.

In a world where so many things are taken completely out of your hands, it is good to know that there is this one vitally important area of your life where you can be almost totally in control of the situation. So, for the sake of your health and your future, be sure that you exercise that control.

CHAPTER SIX

Fit for Life

To many people the word 'exercise' brings back memories –
not always happy ones – of PT classes in the school play-
ground or gymnasium. There may be painful recollections of
being made to perform 'physical jerks' outside on a freezing
cold morning or a sweltering summer afternoon. Yet we are
living in a time when exercise has become for some almost a
religion – certainly an essential part of life.

Before you insist that you have no time – and certainly no
inclination to indulge in any form of exercise, please stop and
think for a while. This chapter is not advocating that you
become a fitness fanatic who takes a masochistic delight in
running all the way through the pain barrier to reach
exhaustion. But if you lead a high-pressured existence and if
you feel that you are particularly subject to stress and tension
in your daily life, then exercise can indeed be a life-saver.

Physical fitness is in fact a great protection against stress
and stress-related illness. The very best way of attaining physical fitness is by regular exercise. By making exercise a part
of your life you will be strengthening the muscles around
your heart, improving the quality and capacity of your
breathing, encouraging your circulation to work efficiently,
and helping yourself to feel good in the process. Of course
this does not mean that you are then free to smoke, eat and
drink too much, and allow yourself to succumb to the
pressures of your job with impunity. What it does mean is
that those pressures are far less likely to have an effect upon
your physical health.

There is one very important point to make at this juncture. If you have a job which involves a certain amount of competition, it is not advisable to involve yourself in too much competitive sport in your free time – or certainly not to allow it to play too large a part. So many people spend their days striving to do better than their competitors in other companies, or to be chosen for promotion above others in their own company, filling their lives with the belief that they must do better than anyone else. And when they come home, what do these people do? They go straight out and compete on the squash court or on the golf course. All they are doing is exchanging one form of competition for another, one form of stress for another.

This does not mean that you should not feel free to enjoy a round of golf, a game of squash or any other sport that may appeal to you – but keep things in proportion. See the game for what it is – a game. If you win, then that is a bonus. If, however, you find that the winning becomes all-important to you, to the extent that you are becoming tense and anxious about it, then you would do well to find some other form of activity.

Even if you find that you can cope with a certain amount of competitive sport in your leisure time, and even if that sport provides you with sufficient exercise to maintain physical fitness, it is still a good idea to make sure that you have some sort of hobby or pastime which is relaxed and quiet. Perhaps you can enjoy painting, reading, gardening, listening to music, or any other way of spending your time which does not involve you in mental anxiety as well as physical activity.

The best form of exercise for maintaining physical fitness is that which is both regular and controlled. All your bodily processes will thus be improved, particularly your breathing patterns and your circulation. Even a basically healthy individual will be subject to progressive physical deterioration if he takes no exercise whatsoever. It is obvious, therefore, that if your physical condition is improved, you will be better able to cope with any form of stress which may come your way – whether it be physical, mental or emotional.

Just as your mental state can cause physical tension, so can muscular tension influence your mental and emotional state. Since we are all called upon to deal with unexpected and unwanted external pressures from time to time, the least we can do is to try and minimise any possible harmful effects from those pressures by being physically fit.

It has now also been proved beyond any doubt that, all other things being equal, a person who takes regular and controlled exercise performs better in tests which require mental agility. So, by becoming fitter physically you will not just be improving your health, fitness and resistance to stress, but you will actually be better at making decisions and your job performance is likely to improve considerably.

When you exercise, your circulation improves and the amount of lactic acid in your body is reduced. Lactic acid is produced by shallow and incorrect breathing; it causes feelings of mental and physical exhaustion and brings about an inability to concentrate. In addition, there is an increase in your output of adrenalin immediately after exercise and this in turn creates a feeling of general well-being. You must have heard those who take regular exercise claim that they feel 'high' immediately afterwards and that their spirits are lowered if they are forced to miss their chosen activity for even a few days. This is because they have become used to that boost of adrenalin and the good feeling it gives, and they are extremely aware of the lack of it when it is not produced.

Psychologists have consistently found that regular exercise in a form you enjoy lessens depression, improves feelings of self-confidence and reduces anxiety. Indeed, Dr Robert Brown of the University of Virginia insists that he has never had as a patient a person who was at the same time depressed, yet physically fit.

Regular and *controlled* are the keywords when talking about exercise for optimum benefit. There is no point at all in doing nothing whatsoever for six days and then going for a two-hour run once a week. You will, in fact, do yourself far more harm than good. Periods of intense physical activity followed by periods of none at all can cause damage to your muscles and ligaments. Even more importantly, it will do nothing to increase the strength of your heart muscles, instead it will put a strain on them once a week from which it will take the rest of the week to recover! For physical exercise to be of real benefit, you need to work at it for about twenty minutes three times a week. Of course, you can do more if you wish.

Exercise should be something that you enjoy and not something that you have to force yourself to do. There is no point in jogging for twenty minutes a day if jogging is something you find boring and tedious. Perhaps you are one of those people who would be happier swimming or cycling? Indeed, if you have a family, such forms of exercise can often become a shared interest, helping to increase a sense of togetherness and a family spirit, which in turn is a buffer against the effects of stress at work.

There are those who prefer to exercise alone and those who prefer company. Perhaps you would enjoy your physical activity more in a class or group situation? Perhaps you would like the company of just one person? Or perhaps you would prefer to walk, run, or swim on you own? Do whatever pleases you most or you will never stick to it.

Of course you do not have to take the same form of exercise on each occasion. There is no harm at all in taking the family to the swimming pool at the weekend and performing an exercise routine on your own two or three times during the week. Find the method which suits you and your own particular lifestyle.

Start slowly. If you have not indulged in any form of regular physical exercise for some time, it is vitally important to take things slowly to begin with. Indeed, if you feel that you are physically unfit – or if you have any known medical condition – it seems only sensible to have a check-up before you embark on a programme of physical exercise. At the end of this chapter you will find a programme of simple stretching and warming-up exercises which you can practise at home if you feel that you are not yet ready to try anything more energetic.

Exercise can be both enjoyable and beneficial. It does not have to be agony, nor does it have to leave you feeling physically and mentally exhausted. Take things at a gentle and steady pace and do not overdo it. You should still be able to hold a normal conversation after a period of exercise. If you cannot, then you may be over-taxing yourself and you would be well advised to take things more gently.

Exercise and Your Heart

Heart attacks are becoming more and more frequent in our 'civilised' Western world. It is now medically acknowledged that those who exercise regularly are less likely than others to suffer a heart attack. Even among those who have had heart attacks in the past, exercise can go a long way towards preventing a recurrence, although in this case the exercise should always be supervised – at least to begin with. The right sort of exercise can increase the tone of the muscles of the heart and can improve the condition of the heart itself.

Heart attacks and angina occur when the coronary blood vessels become blocked by blood clots or fatty deposits. Regular exercise helps to expand these coronary blood vessels so that this blockage is far less likely to happen. It also reduces the tendency of the blood to form unwanted clots.

Blood pressure too can be reduced by controlled and steady periods of exercise. Since those people who are susceptible to stress are likely to have a higher than desirable blood pressure, this can only be beneficial. It means that while you are going through the process of re-adjusting your lifestyle, you can reduce the harmful effects of stress by exercising regularly. Isometric exercises – which have a purpose to serve in improving muscle tone – do not develop and improve your breathing and can actually increase tension, so these should be avoided by anyone who is subject to stress from other areas.

The chart which follows lists many of the most popular sports and forms of exercise. It also indicates, on a scale of 1 to 10, the exercise value of each individual one. Look down that list and find your own favourite activity. If it has a value of 5 or more, then pursuing that activity for three twenty-minute sessions a week should provide sufficient physical exercise to maintain the basic fitness level desired. If the score on the chart is less than 5, then you will know that you need to increase either the amount of time spent or the frequency of your chosen activity.

There are two important points to be taken into account:

1.   The assumption is being made that you are fit enough to follow your particular sport or exercise enthusiastically and without doing yourself any harm.

2.   This is a chart relating to physical benefits only and does not take into account any stress factor caused by elements of competition.

	1	2	3	4	5	6	7	8	9	10
Archery			——3.5							
Badminton				——4.75						
Basketball						——6.95				
Billiards	——2									
Bowling (ten pin)	——3									
Cricket				——4.5						
Cycling								——8		
Fencing								——8.5		
Fishing	——2									
Football								——8.25		
Golf		——2.75								
Gymnastics							——7.5			
Horse Riding			——4							
Ice Skating							——7.5			
Judo										——10
Roller Skating							——7.5			
Rowing									——9.5	
Skipping								——8.5		
Squash									——9.5	
Swimming									——9.5	
Table Tennis	——3									
Tennis					——5.75					
Water Skiing					——5.25					
Walking, Running:										
1 km in 15 mins.		——2.75								
1 km in 7.5 mins.						——6.5				
1 km in 5 mins.									——9.5	

The following is a selection of basic stretching and warming-up exercises which are suitable for anyone, man or woman, who feels out of condition or unfit, or who has not enjoyed any form of regular exercise for a considerable period of time. They should be practised for at least a month prior to taking up any more strenuous form of exercise. There are just a few vital rules to remember:

1.   If you have any specific medical condition, make sure that you have an examination first.

2.   Start slowly, performing each exercise two or three times and build up gradually.

3.   If at any time you feel any pain or strain – stop. This rule is equally applicable when you eventually take up a more energetic form of exercise.

4.   Learn to be aware of your breathing as you perform the exercises. To achieve maximum benefit, breathing needs to be deep and regular.

Exercise 1

Stand, feet slightly apart, with your hands resting gently on your ribcage and your fingers just touching. Breathe in deeply through your nose, expanding your ribcage so that your fingers are forced a little way apart. Hold that breath for a slow count of three and then breathe out through your mouth, allowing your fingertips to touch once more.

Exercise 2

Stand with your feet together and your hands loosely by your sides. As you breathe in, rise up onto your toes and bring your arms out to the side and then upwards, keeping them straight, until they meet above your head. Reverse the whole procedure as you breathe out again.

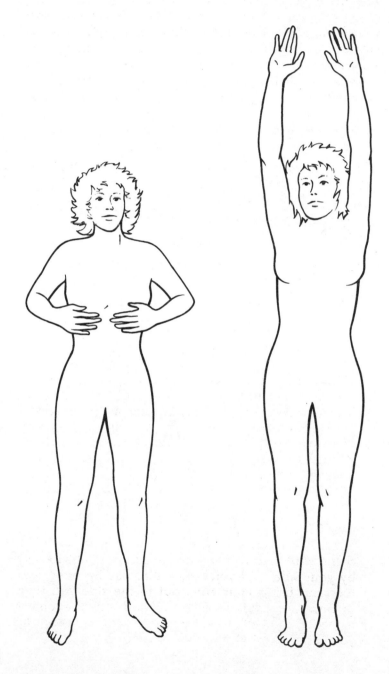

Exercise 3

Place your feet about eighteen inches apart and stand
with your arms by your sides. Without twisting your
body, bend sideways to the right letting your right
hand slide down your leg. Lean over to the right as
far as you can without feeling any strain, then slowly
straighten up again. Now repeat the process to the
left. Remember to keep your body facing forwards;
do not allow your spine to twist.

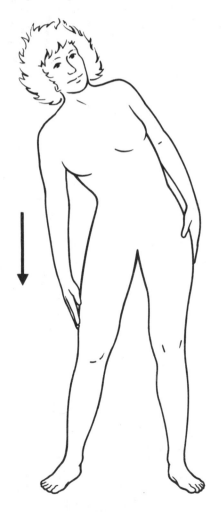

Exercise 4

Stand with your feet apart, arms outstretched at shoulder height, palms towards the floor. Turn to the right, twisting from the waist and keeping the lower half of your body still so that your right arm (still outstretched) swings right round behind you. Turn your head to the right and allow your left elbow to bend so that your left forearm is across your chest. Hold this position for a count of three, then return to the starting position before repeating the process to the left. At all times, turn your body as far as you can without experiencing any pain or discomfort.

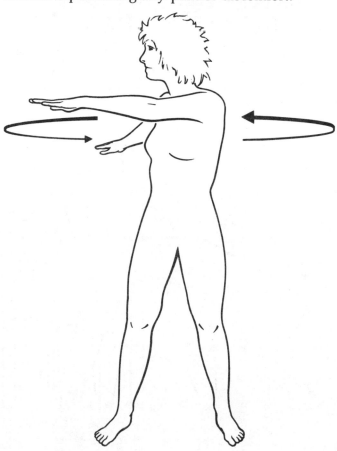

Exercise 5

Stand with your feet slightly apart. Rest your right
hand lightly on the back of a chair for support. Lift
your left leg straight out in front of you, keeping your
toe pointed. Lift the leg as high as you can without
feeling any discomfort and then lower it again. Now
lift it to the back as high as possible and lower it. Turn
around, rest your left hand on the back of the chair
and repeat with the right leg.

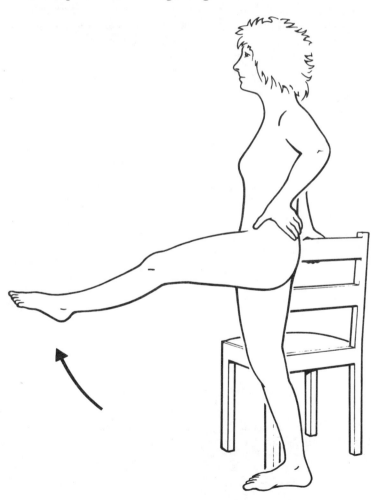

Exercise 6

Resting your right hand lightly on the back of the chair, stand with your feet a little way apart. Keeping your body as upright as possible, lift the left leg straight out towards the side and up as high as you can without feeling any strain. Lower the leg slowly to the ground again. When you have done this as often as required, turn around, rest your left hand on the back of the chair and repeat the exercise with the right leg.

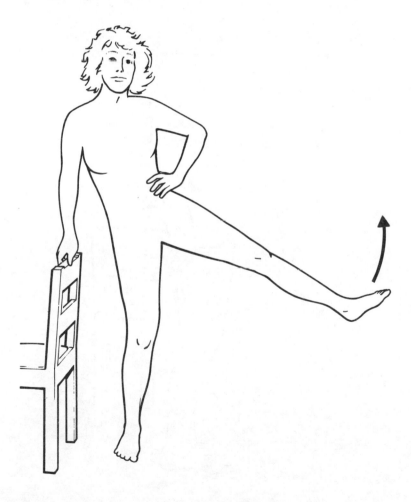

Exercise 7

Stand with feet apart, resting your right hand on the back of the chair for support. Keeping your back straight, bend your left leg and lift it so that your knee is as near to your chest as you can get it without straining. Lower it again. Turn around, rest your left hand on the back of the chair and repeat the exercise with the right leg.

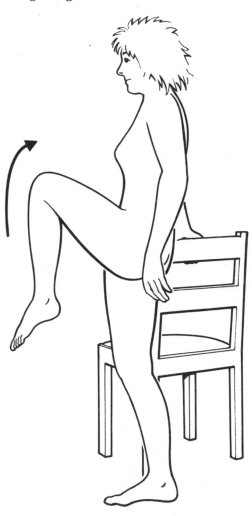

Exercise 8

Sit on the floor, legs straight out in front of you and slightly apart, toes pointing towards the ceiling. Rotating from the ankles, draw imaginary circles with your big toes in a clockwise direction. Make five large circles. Then stop and repeat the process in an anti-clockwise direction.

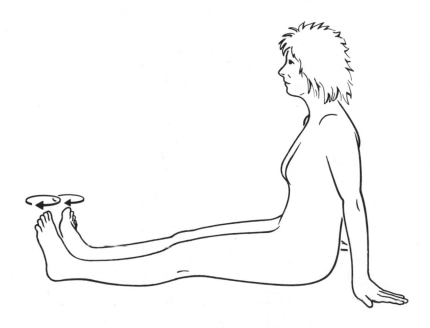

Exercise 9

Sit on a straight-backed chair. Keeping your spine
straight, allow your head to drop forwards towards
your chest. Very slowly raise it again and allow it to
drop backwards. Do not jerk it or you will hurt your
neck muscles. Straighten up again and allow your
head to drop slowly as far to the right as you can
without hurting. Then repeat to the left. Remember
that this exercise should be done very slowly and in a
controlled manner.

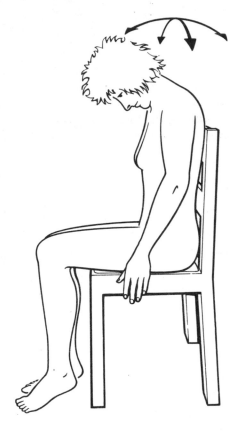

Exercise 10

Repeat Exercise 1

CHAPTER SEVEN

Inner Peace Through Meditation

In Chapter Four, various methods of relaxation were described and hopefully by now you will have begun to practise one or more of them. Now we are going to look at a way of taking things one step further, and of finding that sense of inner peace which will stand you in good stead when external problems appear to surround you. There is no way that you are going to become a saintly figure who is totally unaffected and serene no matter what is going on around you – indeed you would probably be quite insufferable if that were to happen! What we are trying to do is to find a method of putting things in perspective, and thereby preserving your mental and physical health. Once you have attained a state of inner calm you will find that, although you may not always be happy with a specific situation, you will have the ability to stand back from it, to change what can be changed and to make the best of what cannot.

Don't be put off by the word 'meditation'. You do not have to rush out and join some oddly-garbed sect, nor do you have to follow any particular philosophy with which you may not entirely agree. Religion does not come into it at all. Meditation will not affect any religious beliefs you may have, nor will your existing beliefs preclude you from practising a technique which will enable you to make stress a stranger in your life.

Although it is of course possible to practise meditation in a group or to study under a particular teacher, it is also something which can be practised and accomplished quite simply alone and in your own home – provided that you are willing to give it ten minutes of your time each day.

You will find several meditation techniques set out in this chapter. As with the relaxation exercises earlier in the book, there is no one technique which is going to be suitable for every person. All you can do is to try them one at a time until you find the method which is most appropriate. Once you have discovered the best form of meditation for you, try and spend at least ten minutes each day practising it. It is quite a good idea to spend five minutes practising a relaxation technique followed by ten minutes of meditation, as the relaxation can only enhance the meditative period.

Although several methods are set out here, give each one a fair chance. No useful purpose will be served by trying method one on the first day, method two on the second, and so on. Concentrate on each one for about ten days before deciding whether it appeals to you or whether you should reject it in favour of another.

So what is the difference between relaxation and meditation? During relaxation you focus your attention primarily on yourself – on the physical letting go of tension and on the sound of your breathing. With meditation you learn to concentrate on an outside object – real or imaginary. This object can be an image, a word, a sound or an idea. You also learn to become aware of the difference between your internal and your external feelings.

The aim is to observe your chosen object dispassionately, whether you are actually looking at it or whether it is in your imagination only. No thoughts, ideas or opinions are encouraged. You are not being asked to make judgements. You are trying to banish all other thoughts, feelings and anxieties by focusing your attention on this one single thing. This is not something which comes easily or naturally; it takes practice, but if you are willing to give it some time and some effort, the rewards are well worth having.

Those who have made a study of the effects of meditation have shown the various physiological changes which occur. These include:

- lowering of blood pressure;

- slowing of pulse rate;

- improvement in circulation;
- deeper, slower breathing;
- reduction of harmful lactic acid in the body.

Meditation also brings about a change in the electrical activity of the brain which can be measured by EEG. During meditation this electrical activity becomes more even and more regular. This is called attaining the alpha rhythm and it leads to feelings of inner peace and tranquillity. At the same time, there is a reduction in the level of the hormone cortisol which is known to induce stress.

Those who have taken part in my Stress Management Workshops have reported the following changes over a period of time during which they have practised meditation:

- stress and tension levels dramatically reduced;
- improvement in length and quality of sleep; also ease in getting to sleep at night;
- improvement in concentration;
- increase in perceptiveness;
- reduction in tendency towards addiction (to food, alcohol, drugs, tobacco);
- improvement in memory;
- increased sense of general well-being.

In many cases those who meditate regularly have told me that they have also increased their sense of spiritual awareness, even if this was far from being their intention at the outset. This may happen to you or it may not. If it does, and if it brings you that special peace of mind that comes with spiritual awakening, then that is an added reward for your efforts. For the moment we are simply trying to improve your quality of life and increase your resistance to stress.

It is very difficult to measure the reduction of stress in any individual because there is no criterion by which it can be judged. In addition, you are not going to see marked differences between one day and the next – it is only the overall long-term changes which become obvious. This is where the charts in Chapter Two are helpful. Use them to note the ways in which your outer behaviour and your inner reactions are changing as you practise your meditation techniques. Keep a record of your progress and see how your responses and reactions alter as time goes on. How do you feel at the end of a working day, and how does this compare with the way you used to feel? How are your relationships with other members of your family – have they improved? Is there now less friction and more understanding?

Never worry if things sometimes seem to stand still, or even to go backwards. After all, if everyone gave up at the first signs of difficulty, there would be no second marriages, no resitting of exams and no second attempts at the driving test. I can promise you that, as long as you persevere wholeheartedly, you cannot fail to notice an improvement in the end.

Learning to Meditate

The following are all basic meditation exercises. Each one has the same objective: to enable you to reach the best possible inner feeling of serenity in order to cope effectively with the problems and pressures of everyday life, while at the same time, not allowing these pressures to affect you adversely either physically or mentally. Try each technique for about ten days to find out which is the most suitable for you.

Here are a few suggestions which should enable you to get the best out of your meditation:

1. Initially it is probably a good idea to choose the same time and the same place each day. Once you become used to the technique you will then be able to use it when and where you wish.

2. Do not eat or drink for about twenty minutes before a meditation.

3. Do not have any alcohol for about an hour before meditation.

4. Spend about five minutes practising a relaxation technique first.

Method 1

Sit in a comfortable chair, one which allows you to have your back straight and your head supported. Rest your hands lightly on your lap or on the arms of the chair. Look about the room and be aware of the various objects around you. Concentrate on each one in turn. Actually say to yourself, silently inside your head, 'I am aware of the window, that it is open and that the sky outside is blue' or, 'I am aware of the table, that it has a white cloth on it and a vase of flowers'. Listen for external sounds. Become aware of a dog barking in a neighbour's garden or of the sound of a radio playing in another room. The object here is to develop real sensitivity to what is around you instead of just blindly accepting that it exists, which is what most of us do for most of the time.

Now close your eyes. Without wriggling your toes, become aware of the feeling of your shoes on your feet, of the pressure of your hand on your lap or of the feel of the arm of the chair beneath your fingers. If any other sensation comes into your mind, allow this to happen and concentrate fully upon it.

Method 2

Sit in your chair and close your eyes. Concentrate your mind upon an imagined object such as a candle, a book or a tree. Hold that picture in your mind to the exclusion of all others. Initially you will find that other thoughts are bound to intrude. When this happens, do not fight the intrusion, merely turn your attention once again to your chosen object by concentrating on its detail. For example, if it is a tree, what shape is it? What colour are the leaves? What is the texture of its bark? The more you practise this technique, the easier you will find it to return your mind to the original image.

Method 3

This method involves the use of a mantra. A mantra is simply a word or a sound upon which to focus your attention. There are some who believe that a mantra should be given to you, but I always feel that it is better to choose your own. You could select one which has a particular meaning for you: perhaps 'peace' or 'love', or a name which is special to you. You could use a word which incorporates a humming sound such as 'moon' or 'drum'. Once you have selected your word or sound, sit in your chair in a relaxed pose with your eyes closed and repeat that word to yourself over and over again. It does not matter whether you prefer to say the word aloud or simply to 'hear' it repeated inside your head. The object is to reach a stage where you are aware of the sound and feel of the word rather than its meaning.

Method 4

Sit in your chair with your eyes closed. Now focus your attention on a particular colour, any one you like to choose. Try and fill your mind with that colour to the exclusion of all else. If, when you first begin, other thoughts enter your mind, try not to be frustrated by their intrusion. Just let them pass through and then return again to thoughts of your original colour. The eventual aim is to be aware of nothing but colour filling your mind. In the early stages, however, it is often easier to picture an object which is your chosen shade – perhaps a field of green. Gradually concentrate more and more on the green, and less and less on the field itself until the latter becomes totally unimportant.

Method 5

Before you begin, select an object to hold while you sit in your chair. Try not to choose one which is sharp or which will become too heavy after about ten minutes. The best items are those which are smooth or soft. Close your eyes and concentrate on the texture of that object. Try and detach your mind from what the item actually is and focus your attention solely on how it feels to you.

Method 6

Sit in your chair and close your eyes. In your mind conjure up the image of a 'special' place – real or imaginary. It can be indoors or in the open air. See this place in as much detail as you possibly can so that you could describe it easily and would recognise it instantly. As time goes on you will become more and more familiar with your own special place, and will find that simply bringing it to mind will be sufficient to have a calming influence upon you and your life.

In the initial stages of learning to meditate you are bound to lose concentration from time to time, but I can assure you that the whole process becomes easier with practice. Don't try *too* hard – it is a mistake to force an image into your mind. The whole idea is to release yourself from conscious thought, and the concept of 'trying' is encouraging conscious thought. There is a vast difference between seeing what happens, and trying to make something happen.

Once you are used to meditation, you will find that you can practise it anywhere – in a train, on an aeroplane or during a quiet five minutes during the course of a busy working day. Once you have learned to meditate, it is an ability which you will have for the rest of your life. It will give you a sense of inner serenity. This does not mean that you will not feel emotions or be only too aware of the pressures which surround you. What it does mean is that those pressures can only affect you on the surface – so that you can deal with them in the practical sense. They cannot do you any actual harm.

Remember that there is no right or wrong way to meditate.

If a particular method works for you – it is your right way! Any form of meditation incorporates and reinforces the ability to relax, to switch off everyday pressures and to lower your level of stress – and that is what we are aiming for.

CHAPTER EIGHT

Outside Help

The most important path towards overcoming stress is the one you tread yourself by making the necessary alterations to your way of life. Various means exist, however, which will help you to overcome the physical effects of accumulated stress, and indeed, go a long way to help you avoid becoming stressed in the first place. It is possible that you might want to take advantage of one or more of these forms of outside help, and to that end, you will find listed here a few of the more common ones together with some information about each.

Some people prefer to seek outside help while others prefer to do everything themselves. Neither preference is the right one; you must choose what is best for you. Above all, do not put off seeking help because you feel it makes you appear less capable and less competent as a person. After all, if you had a toothache you would consult a dentist. There is no reason why you should not seek the appropriate assistance should you be suffering the very real effects of stress.

If you do prefer to 'go it alone', however, there are various books and tapes which may help you and some of these are listed at the end of the book.

Massage

Therapeutic massage is an excellent aid to physical and mental relaxation. It is particularly beneficial for the many people engaged in business who may well spend quite a large percentage of their time sitting at desks or in front of word processors. Both of these activities can lead to extreme tension in the muscles of the neck, shoulders and back. This in turn often causes headaches or lower back pains as the body tries to compensate for the strain and discomfort experienced.

Massage or manipulation reduces tension in these important muscles whether that tension is a result of poor posture, or of stress caused by anxiety or working to deadlines. Accumulated tension in these particular muscles encourages extreme activity in the central nervous system which in turn prevents you from relaxing, even at the end of the day when you are no longer working. You are already aware of the importance of relaxation as a means of overcoming stress, so the last thing you need is to find yourself trapped on a treadmill of tension during the day, and an inability to relax at night.

Touch and human contact are vitally important factors in our lives – and yet it is something which many people are brought up to avoid more and more as they grow older. Think of the way in which we all love to touch babies and young children. We pick them up, cradle them, hug them, sit them on our laps. Indeed, those children who are deprived of this contact early in their lives – even if they are well cared for in other ways – will often develop symptoms of severe psychological distress, such as rocking themselves or displaying a tragic lack of interest in their surroundings.

Having been surrounded by the warmth of this human contact when we are very young, what is our experience when we grow up? It is amazing how many adults do everything they can to avoid touching each other – and this applies to men in particular. What happens when two men meet each other, even members of the same family? In very many cases they shake hands or slap each other heartily on the back. Perhaps one of the saddest sights of all is to see a father and a son – of whatever age – who shake hands when meeting and parting. Have they really forgotten how to hug each other? Even women, who in general are better at displaying their feelings, will often greet a dear friend or relative with nothing more than a symbolic peck on the cheek.

Perhaps it is the 'stiff upper lip' syndrome which prevents us from enjoying mutual human contact? Perhaps adults are frightened that any demonstrations of warmth and friendship they may show may be mistakenly construed as having sexual overtones? Whatever the reason, it is a sad reflection on society that the majority of adults find themselves unable to display simple human affection for one another.

S M Jourard, the eminent American psychologist, carried out research in this area over a period of years. He found that those adults who are able to give and receive touch freely, actually have a greater measure of self-confidence and a more positive self-image than those who are deprived of such displays of friendship and affection.

Massage can re-introduce touch into your life, and with it feelings of emotional well-being. (In this context we are talking about therapeutic rather than erotic massage – although this can naturally create its own, rather different, feelings of well-being.) As well as releasing muscular tension, it stimulates the flow of blood which brings a sense of peace and tranquillity to your body, while at the same time allowing your mind to slow down and relax.

Therapeutic massage can be given professionally or by any one person to another. The advantage of visiting a profess-ional masseur is that you can be sure that he will have the proper set-up. The disadvantages are the cost, the need to make appointments and the fact that you cannot always have a massage when you feel you need it most. If you decide not to consult a professional, there are a few points which it is well to bear in mind:

1. The room in which the massage is to take place should be warm with no draughts. Choose a time when you can be sure that you will not be disturbed. Draw the curtains and take the telephone off the hook. Keep the lighting soft and not too bright. If you do not have a proper massage couch (and there are some excellent folding ones available), simply put some cushions or folded blankets on the floor.

2. The person giving the massage should be as relaxed as possible before starting. Otherwise the recipient will soon

sense the tension and therefore be unable to relax totally, so that the beneficial effects of the massage are greatly reduced. In addition, if the giver is feeling depressed, unwell or angry, these emotions too will be readily transmitted to the person receiving the massage.

3. The giver should wear clothing which is loose and comfortable, and which allows for complete ease of movement. The area of the recipient being massaged should be bare but the rest of the body should be covered with a towel or a blanket to retain body heat.

4. Massage oil can be used to make the hands move more easily over the surface of the recipient's skin – particularly if he or she has a tendency towards dry skin. It is best to buy one of the many massage oils which are now easily available; baby oil or hand cream are not really satisfactory as they are too rapidly absorbed by the skin. The oil should never be applied directly to the body of the recipient. The hands of the giver should be oiled before – and from time to time during – the massage.

Other forms of Massage – Shiatsu

The literal translation of this name is 'finger pressure' and it is a form of healing which originated in Japan. It should only be carried out by a skilled practitioner as it requires pressure on acupuncture points using thumbs, palms of the hands, elbows and knees, as well as fingers. This is nowhere near as violent as it sounds, and a shiatsu massage may be used to give feelings of well-being and freedom from tension, as well as to cure specific problems and ailments.

Aromatherapy

Aromatherapy involves either a whole body massage or simply the massage of the legs and feet, using in either case essential oils made from natural sources and blended with a neutral base – usually sweet almond oil. Different oils are available for the treatment of different problems and illnesses. For relaxation and freedom from stress, either oil of lavender or oil of juniper are recommended. A qualified aromatherapist, having done a lengthy and detailed diagnosis, should be able to make up an oil especially for you.

Alexander Technique

This technique is able to correct many physiological conditions by teaching the sufferers to hold and use their bodies correctly. The method was devised by an actor, F M Alexander, in the latter half of the nineteenth century when he found that he had lost his voice and was therefore unable to continue his career. So successful was he in curing himself that he later went on to work with other actors, singers and musicians who heard of what he had achieved. Later in his life he trained others to teach the technique which bears his name, so that they too could help people in all walks of life.

The basic idea of the Alexander Technique is that, by developing the correct alignment of the body, it is possible to eliminate many of the causes of pain and ill health. If you think about if, what happens when you are tense? Your body becomes rigid, the muscles in your neck and shoulders tighten, your jaw is taut and your teeth clench. In other words, your body automatically prepares for the 'fight or flight' decision of our forefathers. By learning how you can set about relaxing all those areas naturally, you will eliminate tension from your body, and then from your mind.

This is not just something you should practise at those times when you feel tense. The aim of the teachers of the Alexander Technique is to train you to hold and use your body correctly at all times, and to do so unconsciously so that physical tension is never allowed to build up. This in turn goes a long way towards helping you to free yourself of mental and emotional stress.

Instruction in the Alexander Technique should always be given by a professionally trained teacher. It can be quite expensive as anything up to twenty sessions may be needed. The results, however, can be quite surprising as, in addition to reducing your stress factor, many long-standing ills may be cured and several miscellaneous 'aches and pains' eliminated.

Hypnotherapy

Most people, when mention is made of the word 'hypno-therapy', immediately think of it as a means of helping a patient to stop smoking or lose weight. Although, of course, such problems do play a significant part in the life of any hypnotherapist, it is a fact that about 75 per cent of his patients will consult him because they are suffering from stress in one of its various forms.

This stress may manifest itself in a variety of ways. The patient may be suffering from insomnia, migraine, phobias, sundry aches and pains, anxiety attacks, or any of a large range of symptoms. The basic underlying cause in all these problems is the same – extreme stress and tension.

Far from the popular image created by music-hall hypno-tists, the initial stages of hypnosis do not produce a zombie-like trance state incorporating complete loss of will. Rather, a feeling of deep physical and mental relaxation results during which the patient is fully aware of where he is and what is taking place. The hypnotherapist will have induced this state, with the consent and co-operation of the patient, by talking gently and encouraging muscular relaxation and a regular breathing pattern. The pocket-watch swinging rhythmically backwards and forwards just does not exist.

This state of relaxation induced by hypnosis is so beneficial in itself that many people will consult a therapist merely to experience it and then to learn how to use it for themselves, rather than to overcome a specific problem. Indeed, the whole object of hypnotherapy is to enable the patient to achieve whatever *he* or *she* wishes. It is not possible to be hypnotised to do anything you would not want to do; nor will hypnosis help you to overcome a problem unless you wish to overcome it. Many a smoker is turned away when the therapist discovers that his patient does not really *want* to give up the habit but merely thinks that he *should*.

Naturally, being taught to relax utterly and completely – marvellous as it feels – can do nothing to solve your external problems. What it can do is to change the way in which those external problems affect you, and thereby lessen your chances of falling victim to stress-induced illnesses such as strokes, ulcers and heart-attacks.

It is vitally important that you consult a properly trained and qualified hypnotherapist. At the end of the book you will find various organisations who will be prepared to give you details of established and qualified therapists in your area.

Yoga

Say the word 'yoga', and the image which springs to the mind of the uninitiated is that of someone either standing on his head or tying his body in unbelievable knots. Neither of these mental visions presents the correct picture of what yoga is all about.

The word 'yoga' actually means *union* or *integration*. Regular practice of the technique brings calmness and serenity to the individual, eliminating the negative results of accumulated stress.

According to the theory of yoga, we all consist of three basic 'selves': 1. the subconscious, 2. the intellectual and 3. the creative. Ideally these three parts should be well-balanced, but in many cases they are not. There are some people, for example, who are stimulating intellectually but are definitely lacking in the other two areas. In fact, the number of people who have a natural balance of these three areas of themselves are few indeed, as we have all been continuously programmed and affected by such things as our environment and the people with whom we have come into contact.

This acquired imbalance in our inner selves always causes tension and internal conflict. Yoga works to restore the correct balance and thereby resolve this conflict. This is done be removing stresses of all sorts within the body and the mind.

As well as experiencing physical benefits, once you have learned through yoga to eliminate the tensions of your body, you will find that you have a far greater capacity for concentration, study and hard work. You will not be dissipating so much of your inner energies and so the making of decisions will be quicker and easier for you. The benefits experienced by someone in any area of the business world will therefore be significant.

All you need to give is about fifteen minutes of your time every day. Furthermore, unless you want to, there is no need to reach the stage where you indulge in the sort of physical contortion normally associated with yoga in the mind of the layman. The emphasis will always be on your breathing and on the slow and controlled performance of the exercises.

It is possible to learn the techniques of yoga by attending a regular class and then practising what you have learned. There are also quite a number of excellent cassettes on the market with exercises which have been graded according to the experience of the pupil. It could be that you would be happier using such a cassette in your own home at a time of day convenient to you.

Whatever form of therapy or learning technique you decide to use, remember that its purpose is to enhance and accelerate the stress-reduction which you are already incorporating as part of your everyday life. There is no point in becoming the best pupil in the world of your local Alexander teacher, or of being an excellent subject for hypnosis, if you are then going to let all the old stress-inducing habits control your day-to-day life at work and at home.

CHAPTER NINE

All in the Mind

It would be foolish to pretend that everything which causes stress can be eliminated. But there is one very large area where you can do a great deal to help yourself using the greatest tool you possess – your imagination.

Much of the stress which is suffered in business situations is caused by anxious anticipation: 'I didn't clinch that deal last week, what will my supervisor say?'; 'I have to make a presentation in front of fifty tough executives'; 'I'm on the short-list for a senior management post and I have to face the interview panel'. These and similar apprehensions about future events are likely to instil fear and trepidation in any individual. That fear may well cause him to be severely stressed, and that stress in turn is likely to make him acquit himself badly, thereby making all those fears a reality.

We already know that a limited amount of stress might endow you with that extra sparkle when making your presentation, or give you that extra ounce of courage needed to ask for a salary increase. For many people, however, the stress far exceeds that limited amount needed. It often assumes mammoth proportions and the repercussions which follow affect every area of life.

Imagine young John Brown, full of anxiety because he has a meeting scheduled with Mr Strong, a potential buyer of a new product being marketed by his company.

Mr Strong has a dreadful reputation for sarcasm and ill humour and many a young sales executive has left his office in a state of severe mental agitation. In fact, John Brown's predecessor was so badly affected by his encounter with Mr Strong that he lost all confidence in himself and his abilities, and left the company. None the less, John Brown's boss is very keen to interest Mr Strong in the current product and has asked John to deal with the matter.

How do you think John Brown feels as he waits for the day of the appointment to arrive? His nervousness increases with each day that passes until he has worked himself up into a state of severe agitation and has convinced himself that he is bound to fail in his efforts to secure an order. That in turn will invoke the displeasure of his superiors and may even slow his progress within the company.

Why is John Brown feeling this way about a meeting with a man he has never met? What has caused this anxiety? Is the stress he is suffering justified? All he has to go on is Mr Strong's reputation; he has never even spoken to the man. Yet he is allowing this unknown person to influence the whole of his life, not just his career.

As John becomes more and more anxious about his meeting with the ferocious Mr Strong, he grows increasingly stressed. He cannot sleep well at night, he finds himself arguing with his wife over inconsequential matters, he is short-tempered with his children, and he has a constant nagging headache. By the time the day of the meeting arrives, he is tired and irritable, and is therefore unable to perform as well as he should. So, just like all others before him, he fails to convince Mr Strong of the benefits of the company's product.

Now, of course, he has even more to worry about and an even greater cause for stress. Having failed in his endeavours with Mr Strong, he is less confident in his abilities than he previously was. That in turn is likely to affect his approach to the next task he has to undertake. In addition, he knows that he has to face his superiors and tell them that he has failed and he does not know what their reaction will be. Because his morale is already at a low ebb, he naturally fears the worst and expects a miserable encounter. This puts him on the defensive and makes him likely to bluster and blame everything and everyone except himself which, of course, causes a similar reaction in his boss – leading to goodness knows what outcome. What a miserable chain of events.

Not only will John Brown's business life be affected but his home life too. Perhaps he will feel that he has to 'prove himself' after what he considers his 'disaster' and so he spends more and more time at work, and less and less time with his family. Naturally this is bound to cause arguments on the home front. The build-up of stress, the loss of self-esteem and the extra workload he has allotted himself will all take their toll on his health, sapping his energy and raising his blood pressure. And we end up with one more promising businessman trapped on the treadmill of work-stress-work.

Let's go back to the beginning again. What should John Brown have done when he heard that he had been selected to confront the dreaded Mr Strong? He could begin by analysing the situation and asking himself some pertinent questions:

1. **Why me?**

Just why did his superiors select him, John Brown, to approach Mr Strong with a view to making a sale? Presumably they had confidence in his ability to complete the deal. After all, the company is in business to sell its product; they are going to choose the man they think is most likely to succeed. In one sense, it is an honour to have been chosen as they obviously think he is more likely to carry it off than any of the other sales executives. Not only should that be a boost to John's confidence with regard to the present task, it should also give him hope for the future. If they think more of him than anyone else, having considered his past record, then *he* is more likely to be in line for promotion than anyone else.

So, having studied question one, John should actually be feeling more, rather than less, confident.

2. **What precisely am I worried about?**

Why does the thought of this bad-tempered and extremely ill-mannered man cause John so much anxiety? Mr Strong is unlikely to be physically violent, so the worst he can do is raise his voice, and be sarcastic and generally unpleasant. If he thinks about it calmly, John realises that this boorish blustering is always a sign of insecurity; anyone who has sufficient confidence in himself never has cause to act in that way. It is rather like the bully who invariably is a coward trying to cover up the fact. And John does not even know that Mr Strong will shout and bluster at him; it could be that the last member of the company to approach him was unsure of himself or his product, and so caused irritation and ill-humour in his potential customer. John, of course, will make sure that he knows what he is talking about and will take great care to remain calm at all times. Of course, Mr Strong may still shout and try to belittle him – but he doesn't have to *like* the man, just sell to him.

3. What is the worst that can happen?

Of course, in spite of all John Brown's best efforts, he may still fail to persuade Mr Strong that he should purchase the product. Naturally this would be a blow – both as far as his reputation and his commission were concerned – but would it really mean the end of the world? Provided he does not let it adversely affect him so far as the future is concerned, one failure is not such a terrible thing. It is highly unlikely that the man or woman exists who has not failed at some time. The only way in which such a failure to sell on this occasion could turn into a real tragedy would be if John allowed it to influence the rest of his life by causing him undue stress and destroying his self-confidence.

4. How am I going to spend the time between now and the meeting?

John has a simple choice to make. He can spend the interim time worrying and growing more anxious with each passing day. He can argue with his wife and family. He can drink too much, eat unwisely, sleep badly and wake in an irritable mood. Or he can pass the time making plans and preparing himself for the meeting.

If he chooses the former, not only is he likely to damage his health, his relationship with his family, and his ability to get on with his other work in the meantime, but he is almost bound to fail when he actually comes face to face with Mr Strong. If he does spend the time in planning and preparation, however, there is always the chance that he might fail, but it is far less likely. He will also keep the rest of his home and working life on a far more even keel and he is not likely to affect his health adversely along the way.

Let us assume that our John is a wise young man and has chosen to keep things in proportion. He has decided to look upon his selection for the task as a sign of belief in his ability. He has recognised that Mr Strong is basically an insecure man with no confidence in himself – and this gives our hero an immediate advantage. He has accepted the possibility that, even if he does everything perfectly, he may not make a sale on this occasion. He has chosen to spend the time before the meeting preparing himself for the meeting.

What are the stages to this preparation?

1.   Naturally John needs to know all about the product he hopes to sell. He must be able to answer any question Mr Strong may put to him and to back it up with facts. He does not want to give Mr Strong the impression that he is unsure and inexperienced – that would only give him a reason to reject both him and the product. Of course, it could well be that, when he has heard all about the product John hopes to sell, Mr Strong finds that he genuinely has no need for it in his business and turns it down for this reason. That would not be John's fault, but there would be absolutely no excuse for failing to have all the facts at his fingertips.

2.   Presumably John's business life will go on while waiting for the important meeting and he must keep things in proportion, concentrating on whatever other work is at hand rather than allowing this one forthcoming encounter to override his other duties.

3.   John is wise enough to accept that, even having analysed the situation and decided how he should act, he would not be human if he did not feel some added anxiety when contemplating the meeting with Mr Strong. So he counteracts this feeling by paying extra attention to his relaxation routines during the run-up to the appointed day. He may spend a little longer at each session or he may practise his chosen technique somewhat more frequently than normal. He also tells his wife about the situation so that she will be as understanding as possible and also because any 'ogre' is far less fierce when discussed with

someone else. It may well also help him to keep the matter more in proportion when he hears his wife's reaction.

4.   Finally – and perhaps this is the most important of all – John rehearses the whole situation in his mind. Using the technique detailed in the following section, he 'sees' the meeting in every detail and considers every eventuality, good and bad, which may arise. In this way he has time to plan what would be his reaction in every case, and nothing will be able to stop him in his tracks by taking him by surprise.

Rehearsals in your Mind

Every actor, when preparing for a performance, spends a great deal of time rehearsing each scene again and again. He does this so that he will be perfect on the night. You can do precisely the same thing inside your head, using your imagination. You can rehearse every possible way of playing a particular scene so that you can perform perfectly at the appropriate time.

Let us go back to John Brown. He wanted to give a perfect 'performance' which would culminate in the making of a sale. At the very worst, he wanted to be sure that, even if the final outcome was that a sale was not made, he had done his very best, and that the problem may have lain with Mr Strong, his company or the suitability of the product, but that he had nothing with which to reproach himself. In that way, although he would naturally be disappointed, he would not allow that failure to affect his attitude towards himself or his self-confidence for the future.

So John decided to rehearse in his mind this one-act play with two actors – himself and Mr Strong. The technique is very simple – and extremely effective.

1.   Spend about five minutes ensuring that you are totally relaxed, physically and mentally.

2.   Picture the forthcoming situation in as much detail as possible, John had not actually been to Mr Strong's

premises, but one office is very much like another, and so
it is always feasible to make an educated guess.

3.   Play through the scene as it is likely to be, always
seeing the outcome as being satisfactory for yourself. Now
John would have to write mentally several scripts for his
meeting with Mr Strong. He would need to be able to
visualise every objection the man might put forward and
his own reaction to it. The important part about this stage
of the exercise is to take plenty of time. There is nothing to
be gained by thinking to yourself, 'I'll do it perfectly' – you
need to see in your mind's eye just what you will say and
how you will act. And you need to take the time in your
imagination that the situation is likely to take in reality.

4.   If, in the course of your rehearsal, you come across
something that you would not know how to handle, you
can always take time afterwards to think out the situation
and decide what you would do should that eventually
arise. In this way you will be prepared for anything at all.

5.   Whatever the situation may be, always see the
outcome as being successful for you. Never even entertain
the possibility of failure. This is a time for absolute
confidence in yourself. The Dale Carnegie course has a
saying, 'Act enthusiastic and you'll be enthusiastic'. I
would suggest that the following also applies, 'Act
confident and you'll be confident'.

We are all victims of programming by people and events we
have encountered throughout our lives. Take the example of
the small child who one day drops a cup which his mother
has asked him to carry. The next time she gives him
something, the mother emphasises the fact that he must be
careful, and tells him to make sure that he does not drop it
this time. Of course the poor infant is so terrified by the
thought of dropping something else that he immediately
becomes tense and anxious – and is therefore far more likely
to drop this new item. So his mother starts to tell people not
to give him things to carry as he always drops them. This
little boy is likely to grow up into a young man convinced
that he is clumsy and accident-prone. But he was just a little

boy who once dropped a cup. All the rest came about because of other people.

In just the same way, success breeds success and failure breeds failure. John Brown could either have concentrated on the failure aspect – Mr Strong's reputation and the disastrous results of his predecessor's visit to him; or on the success aspect – his own worth to the company as shown by his past record and the confidence obviously felt in him by his superiors.

He could also have allowed himself to be programmed by fear, childhood fear of all those 'authority figures' who only knew one way of getting what they wanted – by instilling terror in those who were unable to fight back. Such people have existed in everyone's life in the past, but there is no reason why they should be allowed to affect the present, or the future. In the same way that one can re-record over an old cassette, John – and everyone else similarly affected by previous encounters – can re-record over the past, substituting a new and more satisfactory image.

Let me tell you about Sam who attended one of my Stress Management Workshops. Sam had worked for the same company since he was a lad, starting on the factory floor and working his way up the ladder until eventually, because of his knowledge and experience, he had been offered a seat on the board.

Sam was an intelligent man who had obviously learned about every aspect of the job, and he did not doubt either his knowledge of the work or his ability to relate to the men. What did concern him was his lack of academic ability. He had left school at fifteen and started work in the factory almost immediately. Now, faced with board meetings, he was terrified of opening his mouth because he felt that the other members would look down upon him because his vocabulary was not as extensive as theirs, and his grammar was occasionally not quite as polished as it might have been.

As it happened, the other members of that particular board did not look down on Sam at all. They appreciated his honesty and his experience, and it really did not matter if he dropped a few aitches or was a little clumsy in his speech. The problem was entirely in Sam's mind – but this did not make it any less real. It reached the stage where he was so nervous about attending board meetings (in case he appeared what he termed 'a fool') that he became physically ill each time such a meeting was called.

No good would ever come of repeatedly telling Sam that the board members did not mind his lapses of grammar – *he* minded and it was this which caused him such stress. Just like John Brown he had to analyse the situation.

1. **Why had he been selected for the board?**
Since he had obviously not been chosen because he went to the 'right' school or knew the 'right' people, it was obvious that the other members had genuinely wanted the benefit of his knowledge, his many years' experience and his ability to communicate well with the men. They had confidence in him and in his abilities.

2. **What were his options?**
Sam had various choices. He could attend all the meetings but sit there with his mouth shut, contributing nothing at all. If he chose this way out of his dilemma he would be letting down the board who had shown faith in him. He would be letting down the men who looked to him to represent their point of view, he would certainly be letting himself down and he would become an impotent symbol instead of a real participant at board meetings.

If he rejected the first option, Sam could resign from the board altogether. This would also involve letting down all those people and would certainly lower him in his own self-esteem. Or he could continue to become so stressed that he was genuinely unwell on the occasion of each meeting – but then there would be little point in being a board member at all and he certainly would not be improving his own health and well-being.

Or Sam could accept that he had been chosen for his own particular talents and that others obviously considered that he had something to contribute to the meetings. If this were the case, he could prepare for each meeting in the best way possible by assembling in advance all the points he wished to make, by practising stress-release and relaxation before each meeting and by rehearsing in his mind not only what he would say, but the reaction of the other members of the board.

Once he had really thought about the situation in detail, Sam realised that it was a sign of the confidence in him of the other members of the board that he had been asked to join them and that he would be letting down everyone – including himself – if he did not play a full part. Now he had to go on to the preparation stage.

Having worked his way up the ladder over a period of years, Sam was not at all used to the idea of relaxation. However, in his own words, he was willing to 'give it a go'. It did not surprise me, knowing his background of putting his heart and soul into whatever he did, when he dedicated himself to practising his chosen relaxation technique and to changing those aspects of his life which were causing him the greatest stress.

Then he had to learn how to rehearse situations in his imagination – a great change from his former method of 'getting in there and speaking my mind'. Having all the relevant facts at his fingertips was not a problem as Sam was so dedicated to his work that this was second nature to him. He had a little more difficulty in accepting that playing scenes over in his imagination was going to have any beneficial effect whatsoever – but at least he agreed to try.

He decided to imagine a typical board meeting and to begin his visualised scene from the moment *before* he entered the room as he admitted to me that he always found this difficult to do. It seems that he felt as if he did not deserve to be there and that one day he would be discovered for the impostor he really was.

Sam gradually learned to take time to imagine the whole scene as he would really like it to be. After entering the room, he would sit listening to the comments and reports of other members, giving his own views where necessary. When the time came to make his own points, he rehearsed in his mind just how he would behave. Starting by making sure that he spoke slowly and made his points one by one, he went on to 'see' the approval on the faces of his colleagues, to hear their comments, accept their praise and answer his queries. At the end of this scenario he would leave the board room with the others, someone clapping him on the shoulder, feeling part of a very significant team.

I had a letter from Sam some four months after the

workshop he had attended to tell me that, although he would never have confessed it to anyone else, he had in fact been rehearsing regularly in his mind. He was astounded at the results. He had done it because he had made a commitment to do so, but he had never realised that the technique could be so effective. At last he could look forward to the monthly meetings and to having the chance to put his point of view. He felt that the whole of his life had changed as a result and that he had more confidence in himself generally. He thanked me, but, as I pointed out to him, *he* was the one who had done all the work.

If the fictitious John Brown and the factual Sam (although that is not his real name) could use the technique of mental rehearsals to increase their self-confidence and their performance, there is absolutely no reason why you cannot do the same. It takes time, effort and belief on your part – but the results are well worth it.

Think Yourself Well

Evidence in recent years has shown that a great many physical problems are in fact caused by some form of stress. In other words, these illnesses are put there by the mind. There is one important fact that we should all remember: *if your mind can put it there, your mind can take it away*. This fact applies in many different situations – from migraine to cancer.

Remember that we are only talking about those problems caused by the mind. A broken leg is a broken leg and, depending upon your age and general health, it will take a certain amount of time for the fractured bone to knit. There is not a great deal you can do to hasten the recovery.

When we are discussing illnesses caused by stress and put there by your mind, however, there is a considerable amount that you can do – and you can start right away.

There are two important factors to consider:

1. You must believe that you can be well again.

2. Learn to visualise your body overcoming the disease.

This is not dissimilar to rehearsing a situation in your mind, only this time it is your physical condition you are seeking to improve rather than your performance on a specific occasion. The technique, however, is much the same.

Carl and Stephanie Simonton, founders of the Simonton Institute in America work extensively with cancer sufferers. In their book *Getting Well Again* (Bantam, 1978) they explain how the technique can be used to deal with many other forms of illness and disease.

Stress, one of the greatest causes of cancer, affects the body's immune system and culminates in many different health problems. These health problems are then aggravated by various inherent natural weaknesses in the make-up of each individual to produce the disease. To reverse the process it is necessary to alter both mental and psychological processes, as it is a combination of these two which allowed stress and its effects to take hold in the first place.

Three things are required of you:

1. **Practise general stress reduction**: this combines all that you have already learned about exercise, nutrition and relaxation.

2. **Anticipate success**: you must believe that you have the ability to make yourself well again.

3. **Use positive imagery**: it does not matter what form this positive imagery takes. Some examples are given here, but you must adjust your visual image to suit you and your own personality.

Some years ago I met June, a young woman of 32. Although I did not realise it when she first told me her story, she had been a patient of the Simontons in America. Three years previously she had been diagnosed as a cancer sufferer, the tumour being in the area of her chest. Following the Simontons' technique of positive visualisation, she had been so successful that all traces of the cancer had disappeared within nine months and, by the time I met her, there had been no recurrence.

When I asked June what image she had created for herself, she explained that she had been shown her X-ray and had seen the mark on it which was her tumour. Then she was told to create an image which would result in the mark going away. She had decided upon lots of cleaning-women on their hands and knees, all scrubbing away at this mark inside her body. It may sound amusing and unbelievable – but it worked.

It does not matter how 'silly' your visual image may seem to be. If it embarrasses you, you do not have to tell anyone what you are doing. But, like June, once you have seen for yourself how successful it can be, you will probably want to shout it from the rooftops.

Suppose you suffer from severe headaches which are stress-induced. Obviously you will work towards changing your life-style and overcoming stress in general, but this cannot be achieved overnight. What are you going to do in the meantime to ease the pain? Perhaps you could imagine a piece of cool ice on your forehead and, as the ice melts, its coolness spreads over the surface of your head reducing the temperature both outside and in.

This is not something you do just once and then expect miraculous results. While the physical problem exists, you should practise at least twice a day in the following way:

1.   Relax, using your chosen method.

2.   Create your own pictorial image of your particular ailment being cured by your own body.

3.   See yourself in your mind as healthy and without pain.

If you have doubts about the efficacy of this technique, be like Sam and 'give it a go'. Remember the picture does not have to be scientifically based, in fact the more laughable it is, the more it seems to work. However, you must persist, you must want to succeed – and you must believe that you can. After all, you have nothing to lose – and everything to gain!

CHAPTER TEN

Women in Business

Although, naturally, all the problems and difficulties relating to stress which have been referred to so far apply to both sexes, there are some other problems which are peculiar to women.

The last fifty years or so have seen great changes in the lives of women. In the early part of this century many women still did not work, and for the majority of those who did have a job, it was purely a matter of financial necessity. Even then the majority of women's jobs were in the realm of cleaning, shopwork, factory work and nursing, with a few of the more adventurous ones branching out into teaching or secretarial work. The idea of the professional woman with a career of her own is a far more recent innovation.

Even in our present so-called 'age of equality' when more and more careers are open to women, it is not unusual to find that the most senior positions in many areas are held by men. It is still a fact that women have to study harder and work harder to achieve the same status as men, and there are many employers who still prefer to see a man in the top job. Add to this the problems brought about by age-old programming and beliefs and you will see why women have so many extra pressures to deal with.

The items below are some of the more easily recognisable problems with which today's working woman has to deal. They are by no means insurmountable, as can be seen by the number of women attaining high positions in the business

world – or indeed running their own businesses – but they
do have to be considered and dealt with.

Scattering of Families

At one time, when a girl married she would often go to live
just a few streets away from her parents. Probably various
aunts and cousins – not to mention the friends she had
grown up with – would all live nearby too. This meant that,
working or not, when a problem arose or when she needed
help, there would always be 'a member of the family available
to step in and fill the breach. Now, with colleges, universities
and job opportunities taking both men and women far from
the place where they were brought up, it is becoming
relatively unusual to find a young couple settling down in
their original home town. So, should the young woman
become a working wife and mother, she does not have the
security of knowing that there is a loving, caring circle of
people on whom she can call in case of emergency.

Large Communities

Not only is the young woman separated from her immediate
family, but she is likely to find herself living in a highly
populated area. Apart from the fact that this is where the
work is, with the closure of schools and shops in outlying
areas – not to mention the increasing difficulties of rural
transport – living in city, town or suburb is sometimes the
only realistic option. The saying that it is easier to be lonely in
a crowd is very true. You have only to think of the vast
housing estates which seem to be springing up everywhere,
or the miles and miles of 'bedsit land' in London and other
cities, to understand just why so many people seek comfort
in tranquillisers of one sort or another just to survive.

In the days when women did not go out to work, they
would get to know their neighbours as they all went about
their daily tasks. Now, when they come home after a busy
day, it is all they can do to prepare a meal and then either

flop into a chair, do the housework or deal with their own personal social life. As Kay, one of my patients told me, 'I have been living in this street for eight months now and I don't think I would recognise most of my neighbours, let alone know them well'.

Kay lived in a pleasant flat which occupied the first floor of a Victorian house in north-west London. She left the flat each morning at eight to go to the office, not returning until nearly seven in the evening. Those evenings which were not taken up with outings with her boyfriend were occupied with cleaning the flat, late-night shopping or games of squash at the local club. Weekends were the same – only here visits to the family had to be fitted in too. Apart from the man who lived in the downstairs flat, Kay had never got to know anyone from her own street in all the time that she had lived there – presumably they too were occupied with similar timetables.

In smaller communities, although some people would always have the same sort of routine as Kay has today, there would always be others around to forge the links of friendship within the community itself. In addition there would be a mixture of different age-groups in the one area, whereas Kay's street was full of flats and bedsitters occupied by single working people.

Job Conflict

When a couple marry or live together and each has a job, conflict will often arise because of their work. Most couples will start off by agreeing that each job has equal importance, but what happens when there are children and one of them is unwell – who is going to stay at home and take care of that child? In most cases it is the woman: in some cases it is the man. In almost all cases, however, it causes conflict – and conflict causes stress.

The problem does not even have to arise over something as emotive as the health of a loved child. It can be as mundane as the need for someone to be at home when the plumber comes to repair a faulty cistern or the gasman needs to read the meter.

Of course there is always the real conflict which arises when one partner is offered a wonderful opportunity for career advancement, but it means leaving the district to take up a position in another part of the country. Is the other partner going to be willing – and indeed should that partner be willing – to jeopardize his or her own career in order to follow the other to another area? Although in theory this problem could be one which faces either the man or the woman, in many instances it is the woman who is expected to put her career second. Perhaps this is due to upbringing; perhaps it is because in many cases the woman (and who is to say whether she is wrong or right) believes that her work is less important to her than her relationship. Whichever is the case, it leads to the making of a difficult decision, and the increase of tension and stress in the lives of both partners – but more particularly that of the woman.

To Work or Not to Work

Most women will automatically continue to work after marriage – and indeed will want to do so. But what happens when the first child comes along? Then comes the really big decision – should she return to work or not? There is no correct answer; all women are different. But, whatever she decides, you can be sure that she will be made to feel guilty. Of course, before she has even reached the stage of having to make that decision she will have been faced with an even greater one. Should she have children at all and, if so, when?

Jane was 29 when she married Richard. She had been working in public relations for six years and had been promoted twice within the company. At the time of her marriage she was certain in her own mind that she wanted a family, as indeed did her husband, but she thought that there was still plenty of time. She loved her work and knew that she would be able to advance even further. Richard was quite happy with the situation, agreeing that they could easily start a family after a few years. But as Jane's career advanced and she grew more successful, it became harder and harder to contemplate giving it all up.

Suddenly – overnight, or so it seemed – Jane was 36 years

old. She knew then that she had to make a decision or it
would soon be too late to have children at all. Whatever she
decided would be wrong in some respect. To give up all that
she had worked for – the job she loved, the salary which
allowed her a standard of life to which she had become
accustomed, the feeling of being an important individual in
her own right – and stay at home with a child seemed
unthinkable. On the other hand, to spend the rest of her life
childless, denying her own instinctive desires and possibly
regretting it when it was far too late, was unthinkable too.
Not only that, but Richard was beginning to put pressure on
her by trying to persuade her that they should start a family
as soon as possible. He had been an only child and was
anxious that his son or daughter would have at least one
brother or sister.

Rightly or wrongly, Jane decided to continue with her
career and to give up thoughts of a family of her own. She
continued to go from success to success and was on the
surface a happy and fulfilled woman. Only she knew the
pangs of regret she continued to feel during the following
years when she thought of what might have been.

Guilt

The greatest cause of stress in working women – and indeed
in women generally – is guilt. There are some women whose
idea of perfect happiness is to be a good wife and mother, to
stay at home bringing up the family and looking after the
house, perhaps doing a small part-time job which doesn't
intrude on their lives in any way. These women are very
lucky to have found a role in life which suits them.
Unfortunately, however, the world – inspired quite often by
the media – condemns them for the life they have chosen.
They are made to feel that they are second-class citizens or
that they have chosen a subservient role in life. Just look at
any traditional Jewish, Italian or Greek family and see
whether the mother is a second-class citizen!

Women who choose to stay at home are also made to feel
guilty because they are wasting their education or because
they are not adding to the family income. This condemnation

undermines their decision, and causes self-doubt and loss of confidence – and how sad that is. Provided that they have made a choice and are following the career of being a wife and mother, they are to be admired not criticised.

Yet how do these same critics view the mother who returns to work as soon as possible after the birth of her child? She is also made to feel guilty for being an inadequate and an uncaring mother. How could she leave the bringing up of her child to others, however loving and caring those others might be? How could she be selfish enough to put her own career before the needs of her child?

What these critics should realise is that the woman often feels guilty enough without any assistance from them! Even if she believes that she has made the right decision in returning to work, there will be times when she has to leave the house in the morning knowing that her child is unwell or times when she regrets that someone else will be the one to see those first few tottering steps or the first tiny tooth.

Maxine was one of those who decided to return to work when her daughter was only six months old. Much as she loved her child, she could not wait to continue her flourishing career. She had a loving and supportive husband and a good income of her own. She hired an excellent nanny who soon become part of the family. If she did feel the odd pang of guilt about leaving her child in someone else's care day after day, she was able to suppress it. But, as she told me, she felt acute anguish when, on a sunny Sunday in the garden, her little girl had a fall and, bursting into tears, totally ignored her mother, rushing straight to her nanny for comfort.

Perhaps it is the thought of their mothers, who had far fewer labour-saving devices than we do now, which causes some women to feel guilty if anyone should ever find them sitting and relaxing. Although it is a general failing of our times that people think they should always be doing something constructive, once again it is the women who suffer by far the greatest guilt. It is almost as if, because they do not appear to be actively engaged in any particular activity, they must be idle and lazy. Whereas, in fact, everyone is entitled to some time to themselves: to read, sew, watch television, listen to music, or simply to do nothing at all. Indeed, as we have already seen earlier on in this book, sitting and relaxing is an admirable antidote to the stress we all suffer during the course of our everyday lives.

Returning to Work After a Long Gap

For those women who have taken time to be at home with their children for several years and who then wish to return to work, there are also particular problems. Unless they are willing to settle for a job far lower down the scale than that to which they are entitled, they may indeed encounter a great many difficulties.

With the rapid technological development which has taken place over the past few years, anyone who has been out of circulation with regard to the business world is likely to find her skills quite out of date.

Meg started out as a shorthand typist in a large company, and had worked her way up to the position of personal private secretary to the managing director when she gave up work to have, and then care for, her twin sons. She made the decision that she would not return to work until the boys were eleven and had started at the senior school. This was made easier for her by the fact that there was no real financial need for her to work; her husband ran his own successful haulage company and they enjoyed a comfortable standard of living.

In the relatively short space of time between Meg leaving her job and wishing to take up another, the business world had changed dramatically. From a period when to be proficient with an electronic typewriter and a calculator was considered an asset, the business world had become a place where computers, word-processors and fax machines had arrived on the scene. Meg, of course, had not been in an office situation during that time and she was well aware that she had none of the necessary skills for a position equivalent to the one she had had before leaving to become a full-time mother. What made it worse was that her own sons, young as they were, were quite familiar with the workings of computers and word processors, having already come across them both at school and at home.

Meg's confidence was at a really low ebb. Even after a series of evening classes in modern business technology, she only applied for jobs which were far below her capabilities. She actually had great difficulty in getting work at all as, feeling so unsure of herself, she did not acquit herself well in interviews.

Once self-confidence is lost, life becomes far more difficult as you are caught on that merry-go-round of setting yourself low standards and then, because you are aware that you are not being stretched in your work, finding that you have even less confidence in yourself and your abilities. What is worse, even if you do have faith in yourself and in what you can do, it is none the less a fact that many employers are not over-anxious to employ older women who have not worked for some time.

Many women who have raised their children and who find it impossible to find the type of work they feel is worthy of them decide to set up in business for themselves. To start a business of your own, whether you are a man or a woman, takes courage and a real belief in yourself and, of course, this is just what you may not have if you have been away from the career circuit for some time. This is not intended to discourage anyone from trying – and indeed succeeding as so many do – but merely to point out that you must have complete confidence in yourself and what you can achieve. If you do not believe in yourself, no one else is likely to.

Fortunately, the converse situation also exists. Women who have almost been forced by circumstances to become self-employed find that, not only do they succeed far beyond their original expectations, but their confidence increases with each achievement.

Equality?

Even in our present 'age of equality', there is still a vast difference in the opportunities available for men and for women. Furthermore, although pay is supposed to be equal too, this is often not the case.

This doesn't mean that there are not many women in top positions earning fantastically high salaries. It is simply that they are few and far between compared to those who come up against a solid brick wall of prejudice when they seek the advancement and recompense that they deserve.

There are other problems facing the career woman too. Rebecca worked in the wine trade and, having studied and passed her exams, at the very young age of 27 she was elected to the Management Board of her company. She had no problems with status or with money – her salary being exactly the same as for any man in her position. But she still found that she was treated differently by the other members of the board who never seemed able to take her or her work seriously.

Rebecca had no doubts at all about her ability. She knew that when she prepared her monthly report she did it well and efficiently. Yet, when she presented that report at the board meeting, the other members – all of them men and many of them her senior by several decades – did not accord it the attention and respect they could have done. She felt that they reacted as though they wanted to pat her on the head and indulge her by telling her what a good girl she was. Indeed, it was only after several years of attending these monthly meetings that she began to feel that they were taking her at all seriously.

Sexual Harassment

There are two aspects to this particular problem. It cannot be denied that in many cases sexual harassment still exists. It does not have to go as far as actual manhandling of the woman concerned; it may be suggestion, innuendo or even the telling of unsavoury jokes in her presence. If it causes her distress and embarrassment, it is harassment just the same.

Quite often the woman will feel that there is nothing she can do about such a problem. For one thing she does not wish to jeopardise her job. This would be a definite possibility, particularly when the guilty party is her superior. If she makes any protest at all she lays herself open to being called a 'prude' or a 'spoilsport' and is reminded that she chose to take part in the 'man's world' of business.

Of course there are cases where what the woman sees as

sexual harassment is in fact no more than kindness or courtesy. Just as there are some men who feel that it is their right to make suggestive comments to any woman they encounter, so too are there women who are only too ready to construe indications of friendship as a prelude to a sexual approach.

Whether the problem of sexual harassment at work actually exists, or whether it is present only in the mind of the woman concerned, none the less the end result is the same – she feels that she is put under pressure by the situation, and this only serves to increase her stress factor.

Marriage

Look at the following charts. They are based on the stress-factor scale by T H Holmes and R H Rahe in the *Journal of Psychomatic Research*, 1967. The figures indicate the stress factor imposed upon men and women when they marry.

MEN

SITUATION	STRESS POINTS
Marriage	50
Change in financial state	38
Change in personal habits	24
Change in sleeping habits	16
Change in eating habits	15
TOTAL	143

WOMEN

SITUATION	STRESS POINTS
Marriage	50
Change in financial state	38
Change in personal habits	24
Change in sleeping habits	16
Change in eating habits	15
Change in household responsibility	29

Change in living conditions	25
Change in work conditions	20
Change in residence	20
Change in social role and activities	18
TOTAL	255

These figures are taken from the work of Dr Audrey Livingstone Booth, a Lecturer of the Institute of Education, London University.

It is still expected in many cases that the woman will take the greater part of the responsibility for the care of the home – and women themselves are in many ways to blame for this. They feel that it is their 'job' to run the home and prepare the food, even though they may have another full-time job during the day. When – as is becoming the case more often, particularly among younger men – the man wishes to help and to play his part in the care of the home and the preparation of the food, many women feel that they are not being real wives if they allow this to happen. In reality, of course, they are losing an opportunity for sharing and togetherness which is invaluable in the consolidation of any relationship.

There are still some magazines which lead the more gullible woman to believe that she should be a combination of Miss World, Supercook, agony aunt, fashion model, sexual plaything, nurse and Businesswoman of the Year – and all this without smudging her lipstick! Because she is unable to be this amazing person, the woman will feel that she is a failure in some way and this will only lead to added stress in her life. Naturally not all women feel this way but you would, I think, be quite surprised at just how many do – as I know only too well from the workshops I have conducted with women's business organisations.

Difficult Decisions

The life of the working woman seems to be full of difficult decisions. She must decide whether to marry or to have a career – or both. She must decide whether she wants to have children at all – and if so, when. If she does have children, she must decide whether to go back to work – and when to do so.

Suppose a girl has had a good education and has gone on to college or university. She is hardworking and ambitious, eager to get on in her chosen career. If she takes time out to become a mother while she herself is still young, she could well find herself in a junior position or continuing her training when she is in her thirties. On the other hand, if she decides to continue with her career and postpone having a family until she is older, she has to face the fact that she will be approaching pensionable age when her youngest child finally leaves home. Whichever path she takes, there is bound to be a certain amount of anger and frustration – and therefore stress.

A working woman with children who is unhappy in her marriage, will often stay in this unfortunate situation, rather than make the decision to face the responsibilities of her job and looking after the children alone. This, of course, adds to the stress of all concerned; husband, wife and children.

●

Problems Facing the Career Woman

Caroline is a successful career woman. She is married to Keith and they agreed from the outset that neither of them had any desire for children as each wanted to pursue their individual careers. They have been happy together for nearly fifteen years and their relationship is as strong and support-ive as ever. Caroline's work takes her away from home on a regular basis and she often attends conferences and seminars in hotels all over the country. Keith is quite capable of looking after himself and the flat – indeed they have shared all the cleaning and cooking responsibilities from the outset.

Happy as she is in her work, Caroline told me of several difficulties encountered by the successful businesswoman, particularly one who has to travel as part of her job.

1.   There is a great feeling of isolation when you are the first woman to occupy a particular position. Apart from

the fact that you are always aware of people waiting for
you to make a mistake, there is no one to advise you,
should you feel that you need it. Caroline accepted that
she was perhaps at fault in feeling that to ask for help too
often would be a sign of weakness, but she had been left in
no doubt by some of the men over whom she had been
promoted that they were waiting and watching for her
to fail.

2.   As often as she had travelled up and down the country
in the course of her business duties, Caroline had never
come to terms with having to stay alone in hotels or eat
alone in restaurants. The working part of the day never
presented any problem but she confessed to me that, once
that was over, she usually went to her room and ordered
something to eat there. In many cases the only form of
hotel lounge was a bar and, as a woman on her own, she
felt awkward sitting by herself in such surroundings,
knowing that it is still considered strange for a woman to
sit in a bar or a pub alone. She felt that life was completely
different for the men and that she was automatically
missing out on the camaraderie they often experienced,
particularly when the stay was an extended one of several
days.

3.   Although this was not a problem experienced by
Caroline herself, she told me of several of her friends who
occupied senior and responsible positions and yet received
no moral support from their husbands or partners. They,
however, were expected for their part to be totally
supportive and to listen sympathetically to details of
whatever problems their partners might encounter during
the course of their working day.

4.   Caroline admitted to me that she felt her existence was
essentially a lonely one. Although she had Keith and a few
friends, she had never really had the opportunity to get to
know the people in her neighbourhood. As both she and
Keith had jobs which involved being away from home
quite often, and because these trips did not necessarily
coincide, it was difficult to arrange dinner parties, outings
or events as a couple. When she was working in her local

office, she quite envied the typists and the clerks who were able to go out together for lunch or to window-shop. Her lunch hour, when and if she took one, always seemed to consist of essential household shopping.

Fortunately Caroline was a sufficiently confident young woman to cope with the above problems, although she was extremely conscious of their existence. For someone whose self-esteem was lower, however, they could appear a daunting and stressful prospect.

Women in business are naturally subject to all the stressful factors described in the whole of this book. When you add to those factors, all the additional problems they have to face, it is no wonder that so many now are turning to alcohol or to tranquillisers to enable them to cope. Apart from all the physical and mental results of stress already indicated, the added complications of menstrual problems have to be dealt with.

Period Problems

The first thing a woman will ask herself if her monthly period is late is, of course, 'could I possibly be pregnant?'. Following upon this will be feelings of delight or dread, depending upon whether she wishes to start or increase her family or not. Naturally, if she knows that she cannot be pregnant, she is likely to become even more concerned; the lateness of the period has to have a reason and, until she discovers what that reason is, her natural instinct is to worry.

Stress causes muscular tension and muscular tension causes increased pain so, if she is in a high-powered and stressful job, a woman is more likely to experience heavy or painful periods. She then has the added stress of having to cope with this situation while continuing with her business life.

If her periods stop altogether without there being any obvious explanation, a woman is likely to become tense and anxious, even though there can be many minor reasons why this might happen.

Pregnancy

Even when the pregnancy is deliberate and desired, it brings with it various problems and decisions. The working woman must decide how long she wishes to continue in her job, whether she wishes to return to work afterwards and, if so, at what date after the birth she is likely to resume her career. These are never easy decisions, even when there are no financial considerations to take into account. They all add to the stress in the woman's life – just at a time when she should be doing her best to relax.

PMT

Pre-menstrual tension is now recognised as being a real and potentially serious problem which can lead to stress, anxiety and depression. Apart from the obvious physical signs, such as swollen ankles, tight waistbands and headaches, PMT can also lead to irritability and depression. It is caused by changes in the hormone levels in the woman's body and recent research has shown that women are often less successful in both physical and mental tests at this time.

In the days just before a period many women experience a marked increase in their stress level. They become far more anxious and tense, and are therefore even less able to cope with external pressures. This in turn leads them to suffer even more from stress-related illnesses.

In some cases the contraceptive pill is given to alleviate pre-menstrual tension. This does indeed help some women – although by no means all of those who suffer – but there is grave doubt as to the desirability of taking the pill regularly over a period of several years.

Menopause

Reaching this stage in her life can cause a woman emotional and psychological difficulties, as well as physical problems. If she has a stressful and demanding job, these problems may well be increased.

The fall in the amount of female hormones which brings about the menopause can bring with it a certain amount of discomfort and the infamous 'hot flushes'. Although these are not serious in themselves, they can none the less be embarrassing for some women if they happen to be the centre of attention – perhaps giving a report, or making an important presentation – at the time they occur.

The stress caused by the psychological problems can be more long-lasting. Although the menopause is by no means a sign that a woman is growing old, many of them do in fact have a depressing feeling that they are approaching the last phase of their lives. When, as it often does, it coincides with the last of the children leaving home, this feeling is considerably heightened.

As it does seem to mark the transit from one stage of her life to another, the ambitious businesswoman may experience depression if she feels that she has not done as well in her career as she would have liked. It often seems to her that it is now too late to achieve all that she desired.

Problems Caused by Over-Zealous Exercise

Exercise, in the past few years, seems to have become almost a fetish with many women and, although a certain amount of physical exercise is extremely good for you, when taken to extremes it can bring in its wake its own particular problems.

It is not unusual for women who jog, do aerobics, play squash or indulge in other extremely energetic forms of exercise to find that their periods come to a halt. The chemical released by the body during strenuous exercise which induces a feeling of elation, is the same as the 'stress chemical' which causes the body to work so hard just to keep going under the extra demand of intense exercise. So much is used up to cope with this additional pressure that there is nothing left to deal with its normal function. So, exercise is excellent – but moderation in all things.

What should the working woman do to counteract the added amount of stress she is likely to experience? Naturally any or all of the methods already mentioned earlier in this book will be effective, although she may well find that she needs to spend a little more time on relaxation during the time immediately before her period.

Evening Primrose Oil is an excellent way of dealing with PMT, menstrual or menopausal problems. This is a harmless and non-addictive treatment made from pure and natural ingredients and many women have found it to be most efficacious. It is most easily taken in the form of capsules which can be bought at any health shop. It is recommended that a dose of not less than 500mg should be taken for a week before the period is due and then for as many days as is felt necessary.

One of the most pleasurable ways of combating stress is to spoil yourself a little. Indulge yourself with a warm bath, enriched with your favourite oils, followed by the use of a luxurious body cream, taking the time perhaps to give yourself a manicure. Don't say that you never have the time – make the time! It is important for each of us, man or woman, to love ourselves in a genuine, not a narcissistic way. After all, if you do not love yourself, who is going to find you lovable?

Keep in contact with your friends and relations whatever the demands of your job. Even if you do not have the time to see all of them regularly, you can make the odd telephone call, write the occasional letter, however brief, just to let them know that you are still there and that you still care. It will help to make you feel less isolated and certainly less stressed to know that there are all these people around who care about you.

Make sure that you take the time to pursue your own interests in whatever spare time you may have. Life does not have to be one long round of work – shopping – paying bills – back to work. Whether you wish to be energetic and go for walks or cycle rides, or whether your idea of pleasure is to sit back and listen to your favourite music, make sure that you give yourself time to do those things which please you. It does not matter if your interests do not precisely coincide with those of your partner. No successful relationship will be damaged by each partner pursuing his or her individual interests from time to time – and many somewhat stale relationships may even be improved.

The most important thing is to recognise that, as a woman in business, you are probably more likely to experience stress than is a man in the same position. Once you are able to accept that fact, you can prepare for it and ensure that it does not cause you to suffer in any way at all.

CHAPTER ELEVEN

One Step at a Time

Your Checklist for a Stress-free Life

Remember that stress in itself is not always a bad thing. It only causes real and lasting harm when it is taken to excess over a period of time. A certain amount of pressure and responsibility can lead you to greater achievements and therefore to having greater confidence in yourself. But don't forget the choke in the car; keeping it pulled out all the time would soon ruin the engine!

Once stress is aroused, you have two choices: either you must use all the extra energy it produces, or you must set about deliberately dispelling it. In the latter case, pills are not the answer as all they will do is mask the symptoms.

The Most Common Physical Symptoms of Stress

Breathlessness or
  palpitations.
Nausea or vomiting.
Dizziness.
Asthma.
Need for alcohol.
Excessive smoking.
Loss of appetite.

Headaches or migraine.
Anxiety attacks.
Neck or backache.
Ulcers.
Becoming accident-prone.
Eczema or psoriasis.
Addiction to medication
  or drugs.

Craving for food, especially sweet foods.
Insomnia.
Nightmares.
Constant tiredness.
Onset of allergies.
Chronic indigestion.
Nailbiting.
Constipation or diarrhoea.
Finger or foot tapping..

Impotence.
PMT.
High blood pressure.
Anger or violence.
Phobias.
Strokes.
Heart Disease
Cancer.

Causes of Stress – General

Anticipation of a feared event.
Anger, frustration, guilt or unhappiness about past events.
Excessive noise or heat.
Large crowds.
Frustrations of travel – particularly of driving.
Personal or family problems.

Causes of Stress – Business

Heavier workload than it is possible to cope with.
Lack of support from superiors.
Too many different demands made by different people.
Uncomfortable working conditions.
Confusion caused by new technology.
Making speeches or presentations.
Having to manage or supervise others.
Unsatisfactory relationship with colleagues.

Getting to Know Yourself

Remember to complete the questionnaires at regular intervals so that you can see just how well you are progressing with:

- your physical stress factor;
- your mental and emotional stress factor;
- your personality assessment.

Give yourself credit for any changes you have made. Note whether you are:

- Type 1 – unassertive;
- Type 2 – obsessional;
- Type 3 – a stimulus-seeker;
- Type 4 – ambitious.

Then check your lists to see whether you are a Type A or a Type B according to the researches of cardiologists Friedman and Rosenman. Try to become more of a Type B personality.

Set Yourself Realistic Goals

What causes you the greatest amount of stress? Once you have recognised this, you must decide what you will do about it and make a commitment as to when you will start.
    Make problem cards for yourself if you think you will find them helpful.

Change Your Business Life-Style

Delegate where possible.
Change the way in which you travel to work if this is causing you stress.
Give yourself plenty of time so that you do not have to rush and are not late.
Take breaks during the course of the day.
Work a reasonable number of hours each day and only take work home when it is absolutely essential.
Ask yourself how you can get the best out of your employees.

Prepare yourself well for meetings.
Learn to say 'no'.
Deal with each day one at a time; clear the muddle from your desk and keep on it only what you need for the job in hand.
Plan your day; make lists and allow for interruptions.

Change Your Home Life-Style

Make time for your family – you all need time to be together and time for each member of the family to be alone if he or she wishes.
Find a non-competitive hobby.
Don't overreach yourself financially.
Take regular holidays, whether long or short.
Make mealtimes a time for relaxation.
Have a relaxed start to the day, even if it means getting up a little earlier.
Make time in your life for friends and relatives.
Ease your mind by dealing with bills, etc., promptly.
Try to keep your home environment comfortable but un-cluttered.

Relaxation

Make sure that you breathe correctly. Practise the various techniques until you find one that suits you.
Try the different relaxation techniques. Practise each one for fifteen minutes twice a day until you have decided which one you prefer.
Remember to do your relaxation exercise slowly.

Sleep

Put your worries aside at bedtime – there is nothing you can do before morning.
Don't worry about the number of hours you sleep; it is the quality of that sleep which is important.

It doesn't matter if you have the occasional sleepless night.
Reminding yourself that you slept badly last night/last week/
last month is the way to programme yourself for insomnia.
Don't work until just before bedtime.
There is no point in going to bed if you still feel wide awake.
Get some physical exercise each day – but not just before
bed.
Try not to drink tea or coffee late at night.
Don't have alcohol just before bed.
Ensure that there is sufficient fresh air in the bedroom.
Take a warm bath just before going to bed.
Try to establish a regular night-time routine.
A drink of warm milk or camomile tea will help to induce
sleep.
Practise a suitable relaxation exercise in bed.

The Food You Eat

Check the lists of symptoms of vitamin and mineral deficiency
and make any necessary adjustments to your diet.
Try to have a varied and balanced diet.
Buy local fresh food where possible.
Avoid sugar and foods which contain it.
Cut down on fats.
Cut down on salt.
Eat smaller amounts of meat and try to have mainly poultry
or white meat.
Eat more fish.
Avoid ready-prepared meals where possible.
Use more wholegrain cereal, bread and rice.
Drink decaffeinated coffee and tea.
Take alcohol only in moderation.
Spring or filtered water is better than that which comes
straight from the tap.
Avoid those foods which contain too many artificial pre-
servatives. Read labels.
Eat your food slowly.

Remember that there are many things which are beyond

your control but what you take into your body as food or drink is your choice.

Exercise

Take regular exercise, but you don't have to become a fitness fanatic.
Cut down on competitive sport if the competition is causing you stress.
Exercise must be regular and controlled to be beneficial.
It increases your physical well-being and reduces your stress level.
Find a form of exercise that you enjoy.
Decide whether you prefer to exercise alone or in a group.
Start slowly and increase exercise as your stamina builds up.
If you are in doubt about your health, or if you have a known medical condition, have a check-up before exercising.
If you feel any pain or strain at any time – stop.
Check that you are breathing properly while exercising.
To warm up or to become supple, practise the basic stretching exercises.

Meditation

Try each method for a set period so that you can find the most suitable one for you.
Meditate for ten minutes a day.
The greatest benefit will be achieved if you practise a relaxation technique for five minutes first.
Meditation brings inner peace and physical, mental and emotional benefits.
Give it time – you are unlikely to feel any difference after just one or two attempts.
Try and choose the same time each day to meditate.
Don't eat or drink just before meditating.
No alcohol for at least an hour before meditating.
There is no right or wrong way – find the method which suits you.

Massage

Keep the room warm and draught-free.
The person giving the massage must also be relaxed.
Keep the body warm with a towel or blanket.
Use massage oil for the greatest effect.

Outside Help

Shiatsu.
Aromatherapy.
Alexander Technique.
Hypnotherapy.
Yoga.

Control Anxiety

If a feared situation is approaching, ask yourself:

What am I frightened of?
What is the worst that can happen?

Then:

Plan and prepare for the situation.
Rehearse it in your mind, seeing the whole scene as you
would like it to be.

Think Yourself Well

Believe that it is possible to use the mind to heal yourself.
Visualise your body overcoming the problem.

Women in Business: Causes of Stress

Dispersal of family.

Living in large communities where neighbours do not get to know each other.
Having to decide whether or not to work.
Conflict of jobs between husband and wife.
Deciding whether or not to have children.
Deciding when to start a family if one is desired.
Choosing when to go back to work.
Problems of lost career opportunities or influx of new technology.
Difficulty for many women to reach a high position.
Sexual harassment, whether real or imagined.
Trying to do two jobs – career and marriage.
Having to deal with guilt about work and home life.
Desire to do everything perfectly.
Staying and eating alone when travelling through work.
Lack of support from superiors and subordinates.

Symptoms

More women are relying on pills or alcohol then ever before.
Pre-menstrual tension.
Menstrual problems.
Inexplicable cessation of periods.
Problems with pregnancy.

Solutions

Any of the relaxation methods mentioned.
Evening Primrose Oil.
Spoiling yourself with such things as luxurious baths, oils and creams.
Indulging yourself by listening to favourite music, reading favourite books.
Keep in touch with friends even when you do not have time to see them.
Make time to pursue your own interests.

I have learned, in whatsoever state I am,
therewith to be content.

(*Philippians*)

Further Information

Helpful Books:

Chaitow, Leon *Stress-Proofing Programme* (Thorsons, 1983)
Friedman, M and Rosenman, R *Type A Behaviour and Your Heart* (Fawcett Publications, 1974)
Kenton, Leslie *Stress and Relaxation* (Century Hutchinson, 1986)
Markham, Ursula *Hypnosis* (Optima, 1987)
Markham, Ursula *Hypnothink* (Thorsons, 1985)
Meichenbaum, Donald *Coping with Stress* (Century Publishing, 1983)
Norfolk, Donald *Fit for Life* (Hamlyn, 1980)
Simonton, Carl and Stephanie *Getting Well Again* (Bantam, 1978)
Stevens, Chris *Alexander Technique* (Optima, 1987)

Stress Management Workshops

Contact: Laura Vale
           The Hypnothink Foundation
           PO Box 154
           Cheltenham, Glos.
           GL53 9EG

For Details of Teachers and Practitioners

in Your Area:

Society of Teachers of the Alexander Technique
10 London House
266 Fulham Road
London SW10 9EL

British School of Yoga
24 Osney Crescent
Paignton, Devon
TQ4 5EY

Hypnotherapy Register
The Hypnothink Foundation
PO Box 154
Cheltenham, Glos.
GL53 9EG.

INDEX